W9-AVW-757

INSTEAD OF
PRISON

INSTEAD OF
PRISON

BERTHA DAVIS

A GROLIER COMPANY

FRANKLIN WATTS
NEW YORK LONDON TORONTO SYDNEY
AN IMPACT BOOK 1986

Library of Congress Cataloging-in-Publication Data

Davis, Bertha, 1910-
Instead of prison.

(An Impact book)
Includes index.
Summary: Discusses how criminals are charged,
sentenced, and incarcerated, the different philosophies
and goals behind these measures, and ways criminals
are currently rehabilitated outside of prisons.
1. Corrections—United States—Juvenile literature.
2. Rehabilitation of criminals—United States—Juvenile
literature.   3. Probation—United States—Juvenile
literature.   4. Reparation—United States—Juvenile
literature.   5. Community-based corrections—United
States—Juvenile literature. (1. Crime and criminals.
2. Criminal justice, Administration of.   3. Prisoners.
4. Rehabilitation of criminals)   I. Title.
HV9304.D38 1986   364.6'8   86-9221
ISBN 0-531-10237-8

CONTENTS

ACKNOWLEDGMENTS

The author wishes to thank three people who had a special role in the writing of this book:

Ann Kelly of the Cutchogue, New York, Free Library, whose cooperation in making available the resources of the Suffolk County Library System was invaluable.

George L. Proferes of the Suffolk County, New York, Department of Probation, who supplied information and insights, read the entire manuscript, and—most important—demonstrated how a dedicated criminal justice professional approaches his responsibilities.

John Pollok, a distinguished criminal lawyer, whose creative thinking about the criminal justice system triggered the whole enterprise.

Quoted material on pp. 11-12 is courtesy of
WNET/Thirteen and The MacNeil Lehrer News Hour.

Cartoon on p. 21 is reproduced by permission of
Bill Mauldin and Wil-Jo Associates, Inc.

Charts and crime statistics on pp. 32-37 are reprinted
with permission of the Institute for Contemporary
Studies. Sources: Brian Forst, Judith Lucianovic, and
Sarah Cox, *What Happens after Arrest?* (Washington,
D.C.: Institute for Law and Social Research, 1977);
Kathleen Brosi, *A Cross-City Comparison of Felony
Case Processing* (Washington, D.C.: Institute for Law
and Social Research, 1979); Federal Bureau of In-
vestigation, *Uniform Crime Reports* (Washington,
D.C.: U.S. Govt. Printing Office, 1980); Bureau of Crimi-
nal Statistics, *Adult Felony Arrest Dispositions*
(Sacramento, Calif.: 1981); Mary A. Toborg, *Pretrial
Release: A National Evaluation of Practices and Out-
comes* (Washington, D.C.: U.S. Department of Justice,
1981); Barbara Boland, Elizabeth Brady, Herbert Tyson,
and John Bassler, *The Prosecution of Felony Arrests*
(Washington, D.C.: Institute for Law and Social
Research, 1983).

Agreement on pp. 88-89 is reprinted with permission
from the Vera Institute of Justice, New York City
Community Service Sentencing Project.

Survey on pp. 113-119 is reprinted in revised form
with permission from the Missouri Board of
Probation and Parole.

Form on pp. 120-123 is reprinted with permission
of the American Bar Association.

Diagrams by Vantage Art, Inc.

Photographs courtesy of
AP/Wide World: pp. 18, 42, 80, 85, 92, 109;
Sally Pettibon/Sarasota Herald-Tribune: p. 61;
Susan Greenwood, The New York Times: p. 64.

INSTEAD OF PRISON

FOREWORD

As the television camera panned over the huge gymnasium, a bizarre scene emerged: a wall to wall sea of cots and in them, on them, and around them a swarm of men—men sleeping, men staring into space, men drifting aimlessly. And at widely spaced intervals, men in uniform, watching.

"These men," the voice-over commentary began, "are waiting to go to prison. They all have boon convicted of crimes; they all have been sentenced. But there is no room for them in the Tennessee prison system."

As the program continued the prisoners who were interviewed voiced their frustration: "It's all right if you like being around a bunch of crazy people. You have to sit on top of your things because they get stolen." "And then they got people in here that raped their own kids and stuff." Prison staff and public officials explained how the prison space crisis had come about and what would have to be done to correct it.

The governor of the state ended the program with this frank admission: "There is no political gain in corrections. The people of the state aren't that interested in it. You've got to persuade people to spend money on something they don't want to spend money on (prisons), to meet standards they don't agree with for the benefit of people they're mad at."

This is a book about doing something for criminals we're mad at, but not about building bigger and better prisons to house them. It's about punishing some of them in ways other than prison.

But be warned. The proposal that we do anything about criminals other than lock up more of them makes many law-abiding citizens almost as mad at the proposers as they are at the criminals. So, as you turn the page, you enter an area of controversy.

CHAPTER ONE

SHOULD ANYBODY
GO TO PRISON?

Bob took part in a conspiracy to import and distribute cocaine. Calvin damaged a Minuteman 2 missile silo with a jackhammer. Dave shot and wounded his former girlfriend after their breakup. Edward sold classified military information to a foreign country. Henry, driving while intoxicated, struck and killed a young man. John, an officer in a chain of banks, stole $30 million from them. Marie bought furniture for her apartment by writing checks that she knew were no good. Peter stole plumbing fixtures from an abandoned apartment building. Richard shot and killed his terminally ill wife. Stephen sexually abused and robbed five women in a midtown office building of a major city. Terry took a wallet from a drunk who turned out to be a decoy police officer.

Each of these acts is a crime. They are real crimes; they were committed by real people. Federal or state laws establish penalties for these crimes. Peter and Terry, if convicted of their offenses, face jail; the others, if convicted, face prison terms. Both jails and prisons are places of incarceration, that is, places where people are confined. Jails are local places of incarceration. They serve a number of different purposes, but essentially they are intended to hold offenders convicted of minor crimes (misdemeanors), for which the penalty is less than one year of confinement. Prisons, federal and state, hold offenders convicted of serious crimes (felonies), for which the penalty is a year or more of confinement. In this book the word *prison* will often refer to both jail and prison; it will be clear from the context when this is the case.

Which of the offenders introduced above should go to prison? Not a fair question, of course, because no information has been given about their criminal records or about the circumstances under which their crimes took place. You will learn more about them later.

It is reasonable, however, to raise four more general questions. (They have no right or wrong answers.) What is your immediate reaction to each of the following questions:

1. First, the question implied by the title of this chapter: Should we *ever* use prison as a punishment for crime? Yes or no?

2. Should convicted criminals ever be sent to prison *for their own good*, that is, to rehabilitate them (turn them into responsible, law-abiding citizens)? Yes or no?

3. Should convicted criminals ever be sent to prison *simply for the good of society*, that is, to keep them from committing other crimes or to discourage other people from doing the same? Yes or no?

4. Should *all* convicted criminals—no exceptions—go to prison for the good of society? Yes or no?

These questions, given to a fairly large number of people from different parts of the United States would be likely to produce results along the following lines. There would probably be some positive answers to question 2 (about imprisonment for an offender's own good), because some people believe that prison can rehabilitate criminals. Question 3 (about imprisonment for the good of society) would undoubtedly trigger a very large number of positive responses. Positive answers to question 4 (about imprisoning all convicted criminals) would probably be relatively few; these would reflect the conviction, strongly held by some, that getting tough with criminals is the best way to reduce crime.

Clearly, only someone who answered no to questions 2, 3, and 4 could, with consistency, have answered no to question 1 (about using prison at all). In a random sample of individuals there might not be anyone who feels that strongly about prison, but there are people who believe that prisons are such destructive institutions that they have no place in a modern society.

Equally clearly, the people of the United States, as a society, have answered question 1 with a resounding yes. Over half a million men and women are now in this country's prisons—about 400 of them—and on any given day hundreds of thousands more may be in our jails—about 3,500 of them. The rate of incarceration in the United States—that is, prisoners in relation to population—is exceeded only by that of South Africa and of the Soviet Union.

Whatever the different points of view revealed by the previous questions, the following statement can be made without fear of challenge: Prison is an accepted present-day way of punishing people who break the law. Notice that the statement says "*an* accepted way" and not "*the only* accepted way." There are other present-day ways of punishing people who break the law.

In order to arrive at some conclusions about the usefulness of "other present-day ways" compared to prison—the subject of this book—the starting point must be criteria by which to judge "usefulness." We must explore why we punish people who break the law.

Punishment has been going on for as long as people have lived in groups. For thousands of years the purpose of punishment was simple—revenge: "an eye for an eye, a tooth for a tooth." The present-day philosophy of punishment is not so simple, and well-informed, well-intentioned people argue over it daily, but fairly broad consensus can probably be achieved on this next statement. We punish offenders who commit crimes to achieve one or more of the following purposes:

1. To rehabilitate them
2. To make them pay for their wrongdoing
3. To keep other people from committing crimes
4. To incapacitate them, that is, make it impossible for them to commit other crimes

Prisons are a relatively modern way of punishing people for crimes. Cells and dungeons have been around for centuries, but the hapless individuals who were confined in them were simply held there until the appointed time came when they were taken out and killed in whatever way was in favor in that place at that time. Often individuals were kept in confinement because a king or some other powerful individual did not like them, but the idea of confining—housing and feeding—people guilty of stealing or killing never entered anyone's head.

The modern prison was invented by the Quakers in the late eighteenth century to provide an alternative to the cruel ways in which criminals were then being punished in the United States—by death, mutilation, flogging, or public humiliation, among others. The Quaker idea was that the offender, locked in a cell, with no contact with the other prisoners, would have time to reflect on his or her crime and sinful ways, time to repent and seek forgiveness. At the end of the term of confinement the offender would go forth and sin no more. The criminal would be reformed.

The view of prison as a place to bring about the moral reform of prisoners later gave way to a more comprehensive goal: Prison should rehabilitate criminals. Well into the twentieth century rehabilitation was the dominant principle in the criminal justice field. Furthermore, it was taken for granted that the appropriate kind of punishment to accomplish that purpose was prison.

Millions of dollars have been spent on prison rehabilitation programs. Those who cling to the ideal of rehabilitation say that we have not done enough and that we have not done the right things. They point out that only one prisoner in ten throughout the United States is doing work in prison that could be the basis for a job outside, and that the waiting lists for training programs are so long that a prisoner who applies may have to wait five or six years. One can readily document the fact that counseling services in prisons are inadequate, and needed special services not available. The over-

The Quaker philosophy of a criminal's reform through reflection on his sins is echoed in this modern-day prison scene in which an inmate assumes the lotus position for meditation.

crowding that persistently characterizes prisons has always been an obstacle to rehabilitative efforts. The serious worsening of overcrowding in recent years has made conditions that were bad infinitely worse.

12/16 It is certainly true that some offenders change for the better while in prison, but too many do not. Too many who leave prison return to prison. So while modern criminal justice theory still asserts that a major purpose of punishing criminals is to rehabilitate them, prison has lost credibility as being the *kind* of punishment that will accomplish that purpose. Alternative-to-prison punishments are increasingly being looked to as more promising.

Rehabilitation certainly had nothing to do with the punishments received by most of the offenders mentioned at the beginning of this chapter. Calvin, who jackhammered a missile silo, received a twenty-five-year prison sentence; Edward, involved in the sale of military information, faces three life-term sentences plus another forty-year sentence. In these stiff penalties the aim of the criminal justice system was to make offenders pay for their wrongdoing and give them their "just deserts," what society believes they fairly deserve. The formal charge against Calvin was conspiring to impede the national defense; Edward's conviction was on a number of charges involving espionage (spying to obtain military secrets). These offenses are considered very serious indeed, and to show that they are considered serious, heavy penalties are written into the law.

Richard, who shot his terminally ill wife, was convicted of murder and sentenced to a long term in prison. The deliberate, planned taking of a human life is also considered a very serious crime and incurs, in some states, the death penalty. If special circumstances make a killing seem less repugnant, the offender can sometimes avoid the severe penalties laid down in every state as just punishment for the taking of a life. In Richard's case, circumstances were not adjudged to outweigh the enormity of his crime.

It is generally accepted that for some serious crimes prison is the only kind of punishment that is just and that adequately expresses how society feels about these crimes. For some kinds of crimes, however, advocates of alternatives to prison maintain that punishments other than prison can win public acceptance.

John, the bank officer who made off with $30 million, was sentenced to two concurrent (to be served at the same time) twenty-year prison terms. A month before John's sentence was imposed, a former deputy secretary of defense received a four-year prison sentence for a cover-up of illegal trading in stocks. Offenses like these are referred to as "white collar crimes," criminal acts related to the offender's job or profession. Embezzlement (stealing money or property that has been left in one's care) is a white collar crime; fraud (use of false statements to cheat people out of money or property) is another example. People have not been as concerned about white collar crime as they have been about acts of violence, yet Americans suffer losses of more than $40 billion every year from this kind of crime; they lose more from fraud than from theft, burglary, and robbery put together.

Not too long ago John and the deputy secretary would have been much more likely to receive sentences of fines only rather than prison sentences. Those who applauded the prison sentences said that these tough penalties "send a message" that a crackdown on white collar crime is under way.

Such penalties are examples of using punishment to achieve a third purpose: deter (discourage or stop by fear) others from committing crimes. As one public official put it, "The way you end corruption, you scare the daylights out of people."

Few matters of public policy arouse as much heat as this third purpose. If we make the penalties for a crime harsher, will it reduce the incidence of that crime? Experts are frank to admit that they do not have the information needed to give a firm yes or no answer to this question. Common sense, and criminologists, tell us that most people would not commit crimes, certainly not serious crimes, even if there were no penalties, prison or otherwise, attached to these crimes; that some criminals are totally indifferent to penalties; and that some criminals weigh the chances of paying a penalty against the benefit they expect to gain from the crime and act accordingly. It is said to be an adage in the criminal world that "If you can't do the time, don't do the crime."

Common sense also tells us that because crime has increased to an alarming degree in recent years, our present ways of punishing criminals do not seem to be achieving the purpose of deterring crime. But this is about all that knowledgeable criminal justice people seem able to agree about as a recommendation for doing better: If we could find ways to make it more *certain* that people who commit crimes will be caught and punished, the *certainty* of punishment is more likely to deter crime than harsher penalties.

When Stephen's past criminal record was examined in connection with the charges of sexual abuse and robbery, it was found that he had been released from prison a little over a year before, after serving ten years for a previous series of rapes. The district attorney assured the public that he would try to have Stephen convicted on a number of different charges, and that he would ask that the sentences run consecutively rather than concurrently. In other words, Stephen is very likely to go to prison for life. Bob also received a long prison sentence for his drug traffic crimes—forty years. Sentences like these illustrate the fourth purpose of punishment: to incapacitate offenders so that they cannot commit more crimes. Obviously prison is the only kind of punishment that can achieve that purpose.

Of all the purposes of punishment, incapacitation is most in the limelight right now. It is the purpose most stressed but also most debated: "Incarcerate more offenders for longer terms." "Incarcerate more offenders for shorter terms." "Incarcerate selected offenders for much longer terms." All these positions have their advocates. A major current issue in the criminal justice field is the proposal urged by a number of highly respected experts that the criminal justice system adopt a policy of *selective incapacitation.* Their argument goes like this:

- A very small number of criminals commit a very large percentage of the nation's crimes. One estimate is that 6 percent of the criminal population commits one third of all crimes. These are the so-called high-rate offenders, offenders who might pull off as many as ninety burglaries (break-ins to steal but without a weapon or violent intent) and 10 robberies (stealing accompanied by violence or threat of violence) per year. The way things work out now, these high-rate offenders go to prison occasionally for some of their crimes but incur no punishment at all for many and perhaps most of them.
- These offenders are, in general, not the ones whom prosecutors are currently going after under so-called career criminal or repeat-offender laws. Many of the criminals being put away for life under these laws because

of conviction for a second or third serious felony turn out to be offenders nearing the end of their criminal careers, getting ready to retire from crime. The high-rate offenders are a younger group—younger and more violent.

- It is possible to identify high-rate offenders if prosecutors have access to their *complete* criminal records, arrests as well as convictions, including their records as juvenile offenders. (This information is not always as accessible as one might expect it to be.)
- Once a high-rate offender is identified, the current charges should be pressed with special vigor; any other crimes the criminal might have gotten away with should be investigated so that maximum charges can be pressed and maximum sentences imposed. This will incapacitate high-rate offenders while they are still in their high-crime years.

This proposed policy of selective incapacitation is vigorously defended as a creative approach to crime control. It is also vigorously opposed. Those who oppose it offer two main arguments. It is unlikely, they say, to bring about a significant reduction in crime. Furthermore, picking out a class of offenders for special handling violates their constitutional rights. The criminal justice system, they say, must be even-handed.

But back to the root question: Should anybody go to prison? Clearly, yes, in the best interests of society. Who does go to prison? Of the real criminals who were introduced earlier, Bob, Calvin, Edward, John, Richard, and Stephen went (or will surely go) to prison. Dave, who shot his girlfriend; Henry, the drunk driver; Marie, the writer of rubber checks; Peter, the plumbing scavenger; and Terry, who chose the wrong drunk from whom to steal a wallet, did not go to prison. They were sentenced to alternatives to prison and will come up in later chapters.

While these offenders were being disposed of, Arthur Torch was arrested for setting fire to a warehouse but he was shortly released. Frank Punk, arrested for a street mugging; George Dealer, picked up for peddling drugs; Irving Hood, brought in for stealing a car; Joseph Jork, picked up for jumping a subway turnstile; and Kevin Krumb, arrested for child abuse, were also released shortly after their arrests.

And during the same period of time an anonymous horde of shoplifters, makers of shady business deals, purse snatchers, burglars, receivers of stolen goods, killers, and more were out in the streets or at their desks going about their criminal business and, for the time being, getting away with their crimes.

There they are—the caught, the uncaught, the caught who go free, the imprisoned, the ones punished in other ways. Who decides who falls into which group? Who decides who gets punished? Who decides what punishment they get?

CHAPTER TWO

WHO DECIDES WHO IS TO BE PUNISHED? WHO DECIDES THE PUNISHMENT?

On May 31, 1984, Daniel was on his way to cash his paycheck when he was hit by a speeding taxi. Taken to a nearby hospital, he was operated on for internal bleeding. As he drifted back to consciousness he was puzzled by the fact that the figure standing near his bed was wearing not nurse's white but dark blue, police-uniform blue. When Daniel left the hospital, he was headed not for home but for a prison cell. Had fate postponed his taxi accident to May 1986, his story would almost certainly have ended differently. What happened?

While the injured and unconscious Daniel was being prepared for surgery, a gun fell out of his trousers pocket. He had no license to carry a gun. About eight years before, Daniel had been convicted of a felony. Under the laws of his state, (1) illegal possession of a firearm is a felony and (2) an offender convicted of two felonies within a ten-year period must be given a prison sentence, with no exceptions permitted. In April 1985 Daniel was sentenced to one-and-a-half to three years in prison.

The true story of Daniel takes us back to the questions raised at the end of Chapter 1. Fate, chance, or bad luck—call it what you will—brought Daniel into a courtroom to be sentenced. A mandatory sentencing law gave the judge no choice but to send him to prison. So who decides what punishment an offender receives? Legislatures, in part. Mandatory sentences are relatively new arrivals on the punishment scene, and to understand why they were introduced and why they are controversial requires a look at the way legislatures formerly established punishments.

Until the relatively recent past the usual pattern of penalties was one of so-called indeterminate sentences, that is, a range of years of imprisonment for each crime. Take a typical street crime in, say, New York City. Victor Victim is walking home late at night. Carl Criminal suddenly jumps out of a doorway, points a gun at Victor, and demands his money. Victor hands over his wallet and Carl dashes off. Victor is shaken up but unharmed.

Under New York State law Carl Criminal has committed the crime of first-degree robbery. That crime falls into a group for which a maximum sentence of six to twenty-five years is prescribed. The law further prescribes that if a sentencing judge wants to impose a minimum as well as a maximum penalty, the minimum must be at least one-third of the maximum. So if Carl Criminal is caught and convicted, he could receive a sentence of "no less than two, no more than six years," "from 5 to 15," "from 5 to 10," "from 9 to 25," or any one of the dozens of other combinations available within the broad range of six to twenty-five years. This gives a judge a great deal of sentencing discretion.

Indeterminate sentences fit the rehabilitation theory of punishment perfectly. Once a judge has set the outside limit of a prison term, it is left to someone else to decide the point during that term at which the offender is ready to leave prison. The "someone else" is usually a parole board. The earliest point in a prison term at which a prisoner is eligible to be considered for parole is set by law—one-third the maximum term is usual—but whether the prisoner is released then is up to the board.

Indeterminate sentences inevitably produce sentence disparity; that is, because judges have so much looway, sentences received from different judges by criminals convicted of the same crime can vary enormously. Carl Criminal, for example, might get two to six from Judge Lenient, but if he came before Judge Harsh he might get five to fifteen. People involved in the criminal justice system are very concerned about this and many ways have been tried to bring judges together to confer on real and hypothetical sentencing situations and to work toward common standards.

The public does not worry about indeterminate sentences because of sentence disparity, but as crime rates began their alarming rise in the 1970s, indeterminate sentences came under sharp attack on other grounds: "Judges are too lenient; they don't set long enough prison terms." "Parole boards are sending dangerous criminals back into our communities when they should be serving out their terms in prison." Sentiments like these, expressed with increasing frequency and vigor, spurred state legislatures to action. More and more of them wrote mandatory sentences into their laws. Most states now set mandatory sentences for those who commit drug-related or violent crimes and those who are repeat offenders.

Mandatory penalties other than prison terms have also been legislated. For example, Roy Repeater's New York State driver's license was suspended for drunk driving. While it was suspended he was picked up again for drunk driving. Convicted of the second drunk-driving offense, the law under which he was sentenced, mandated not only a prison term but also seizure of his car.

Still another point of view has emerged in public and official thinking about crimes and punishments. Just as many people had come to feel that indeterminate sentences gave judges too much room to exercise their own judgment about sentences, many came to feel that mandatory sentences gave judges too little room for discretion. The judge who sentenced Daniel, for example, openly expressed his reluctance to send him to prison.

In an effort to deal with the problems associated with indeterminate and mandatory sentences, a number of states and the federal government have adopted or are considering determinate sentencing, "sentencing by the chart." Typically, sentencing charts do two things for each crime: (1) establish different sentences for the crime for offenders with different criminal records and (2) establish a narrow range of penalties for each offender group from within which the judge must impose a fixed sentence. The chart sentences are sometimes referred to as "presumptive sentences."

For example, under a determinate sentencing system, if Carl Criminal, convicted of robbing Victor Victim, had no prior criminal record, the judge might be required to give him a fixed prison sentence within the range of two and one-half to six and one-quarter years; if Carl had a high level criminal history, the sentence might be a fixed term within the range of twelve and one-quarter to sixteen years.

A determinate sentencing plan may allow judges to impose higher or lower sentences than established by the chart but then requires them to state their reasons for doing so in writing. The plan may also provide that prosecutors and/or offenders may appeal "off-the-chart" sentences.

Parole is usually abolished when determinate sentencing is introduced so that the only way an offender can reduce a fixed term is by earning "good time." Under traditional rules good time is time taken off a prisoner's sentence for good behavior in prison. Some determinate sentencing plans cut down the percentage of a sentence that can bo takon off for good timo.

At this point the reader might well wonder why *trials* have not been mentioned. Judges, courts, convictions, sentences—these words have appeared over and over again. Is not the principal business of judges to preside over trials to determine the guilt or innocence of accused persons? Absolutely not. True, this is the aspect of courts' and judges' work that is shown on the screen and written up in the press. But actually the major function of courts and judges is to decide what to do with convicted offenders, offenders convicted not by trials but because they pleaded guilty.

Back to the city street where Carl Criminal robbed Victor Victim at gun point. Will Carl be arrested? Probably not. He might be if Victor recognizes Carl; if, just as Carl rushes off, Walter Witness calls from a window, "I know that guy who robbed you"; if a car picks Carl up as he leaves the scene and either Victor or Walter get the license plate number; or if, while the robbery is in progress, a police officer appears on the scene. Without recognition, witness, evidence, or police presence, an arrest in a robbery case like this is unlikely. Carl may well become, as far as this robbery is concerned, one of the uncaught.

Of course the police have many methods of tracking down offenders who commit serious crimes. They rely heavily on informers within the criminal community and on tips received in response to appeals for community cooperation or offers of rewards. Stephen, the office building sex offender and robber, was picked up because a security employee in one of the buildings remembered a series of similar crimes that had taken place several years before. The investigation triggered by that lead took the police to Stephen's door. The fact remains, however, that only about 20 percent of reported crimes result in an arrest.

Even this small percentage means thousands of felony arrests each year. What happens then? If 100 individuals are arrested for felony offenses, it might be expected that 100 offenders will be charged with felonies. Actually, crime statistics show that the following is likely to happen:

100	felony arrests
−35	found to belong in the juvenile justice system
65	
−25	turned over to the courts that handle misdemeanors, or whose cases are thrown out
40	accepted by the prosecutor (usually called the district attorney) to be considered for felony charges

Why does the prosecutor not bring charges against, take to trial, and try for conviction and punishment of all sixty-five? Because some of the sixty-five cases the prosecutor would put together would be so weak that a judge would dismiss them before they got near the trial stage.

What makes cases weak? Consider the following. In a surprising number of felony arrests the offender is someone the victim knows. Little Larry

Wimp and Big Bill Bruiser may get into a roaring argument on Saturday night, so roaring that neighbors call the police, who arrive to find Big Bill beating up Little Larry and loudly declaring his intention to break Larry's neck. On Larry's complaint, Big Bill is arrested for assault. But the case never gets off the ground, for the district attorney knows that a week later Larry will give up any thought of causing trouble for good old Bill. Sometimes fear rather than return to amiability makos complainants back down—fear of retaliation or fear that something in their own lives that they want to hide might come to light if they press a case. Whatever the reasons, noncooperation of complainants is one of the major causes of dropped cases, and not just assault cases, but also cases involving crimes like burglary, robbery, and rape.

Cases that start out looking solid may weaken as time passes. Witnesses who were sure about an identification when they looked at the mug books can not make a positive ID from a line-up. There may have been poor police work: failure to get names of witnesses or failure to hold onto and label the weapon used in a crime. If evidence gets lost, the case may fall apart. If the gun that fell out of Donald's trousors pocket had been swept away, there would have been no case against him.

So in the prosecutor's office strong cases are chosen for prosecution rather than weak cases, serious crimes rather than less serious ones, repeat offenders over first offenders. Clearly, prosecutors are a key part of the answer to the basic question of who gets punished. They have the power to proceed against an offender or to drop the case.

Going back to the account of 100 felony arrests, we see the prosecutor has decided to work on 40 cases. Here is what the crime statistics say is likely to happen to them:

40	cases being considered by the district attorney
−2	"jump bail," that is, having been released on bail after their arrest, simply do not appear in court when called
38	
−4	cases dismissed by the judge at the first hearing because they are not thought to warrant formal charges
34	individuals charged with crimes

Notice that the final number 34 is labeled "individuals charged with crimes." All the original 100 arrests were for crimes classified as felonies. Why, then, is the label not "individuals charged with felonies"? Because between their arrest and their formal charging before a judge, a process known as plea bargaining took place. Here is how it works.

When Harry and James were arrested in connection with the drug-induced death of David Kennedy, the twenty-eight-year-old son of Robert F. Kennedy, they were charged with the crime of selling cocaine to David Kennedy. That crime, under Florida law, carries the mandatory penalty of a fifteen-year prison term. The cases never went to trial, however. Instead, plea bargain agreements were negotiated between defense attorneys for the two accused men and the Florida prosecutors. Under those plea bargains the selling charges were dropped and the defendants pleaded "no contest"—and were therefore automatically convicted—on a much less serious charge, that of "conspiracy to sell" cocaine. The penalty agreed to in both bargains was eighteen months of probation.

In other words, in the process of plea bargaining,

the prosecutor agrees to a reduction of charges, the offender agrees to plead guilty or no contest to a lesser charge or charges, a trial is avoided, and the defendant receives a lesser sentence than if he or she had been convicted in a trial on the original charges.

Crime statistics indicate that of the 34 individuals who remain in the tracking of 100 typical felony arrests, most will be involved in the plea-bargaining process. The majority will agree to plead guilty to a misdemeanor; a few will not get such good bargains but will agree to plead guilty to a less serious felony than the one for which they were arrested; a few will insist on a trial on the charges for which they were arrested. In other words, crime statistics indicate that this is what is likely to happen to the thirty-four:

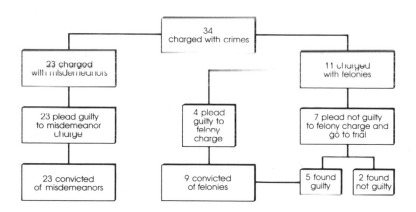

Do not think of the offenders as helpless victims in this process. Attorneys—their own or court-appointed attorneys if they cannot afford their own—do the bargaining for them; the judges know what is going on, and offenders know that prosecutors, wary of trials, will pay a pretty good price in charge and penalty reductions to avoid the risk of cases falling apart in the hands of juries.

As the result of trials or plea bargaining, there were thirty-two convicted criminals to be sentenced. Most of the judges who did the sentencing received a presentence report on each offender to help them decide on an appropriate sentence. Ideally, a presentence report gives a judge a complete picture of the offender: educational achievements and handicaps, family situation, employment history, personal characteristics, relationships with people in the community, and any special handicapping problems such as drug or alcohol abuse. Depending upon the state in which the report is written, it may or may not be accompanied by (1) recommendations concerning the sentence, (2) a statement from the offender's attorney based upon review of the report, and (3) a statement from the victim of the offense. Unfortunately for offenders, presentence reports vary enormously in quality and usefulness.

According to the statistics, here is what the thirty-two sentences probably were:

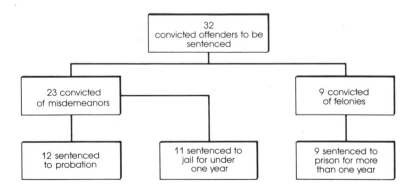

In other words, twenty were incarcerated and twelve given the alternative sentence of probation.

Proponents of alternatives to prison would prefer a much lower number of incarcerations and a much higher number of alternative sentences; nowadays they are not alone in that preference. As a matter of fact, almost everyone involved in the criminal justice system, as well as many other thoughtful public officials, wants judges to "think alternatives." Why this is so is the subject of Chapter 3.

CHAPTER THREE

THE GROWING MANDATE
TO USE
ALTERNATIVES TO PRISON

Picture within a room in your home or school an area of 60 square feet (5.6 sq. m), perhaps a space 5 by 12 feet (152 x 366 cm). Imagine that area as the space within which you spend all your nights and many daytime hours too. Then consider these facts: (1) According to the American Correctional Association, 60 square feet is the minimum amount of space that should be provided for each prison inmate during those hours when he is confined to his cell. (2) A recent survey found that 65 percent of the inmates in state and federal prisons are in institutions that do not meet that standard.

Nobody questions the fact that the prisons of the United States are overcrowded as a result of the rise in crime rate and accompanying rise in prison population that characterized the 1970s and early 1980s. The term *baby boom* comes up frequently in explanations of these two developments, a term that refers to the sharp rise in the birth rate that characterized the period after the end of World

War II. During the 1970s the babies of that post-World War II baby boom moved into the age bracket eighteen to twenty-five, from which traditionally comes the heaviest percentage of criminal offenders. But the baby-boom explanation of rising crime does not, alone, explain the startling rise in the prison population. The longer sentences that were—and still are—being imposed in many courts, the mandatory sentence legislation, and the curbing of parole referred to in Chapter 2 also had a significant impact on prison numbers.

Responses to prison overcrowding have differed from state to state. In some states public opinion has supported the position that if it takes more prisons to get criminals off the streets, the government should build more prisons. Prison construction has been booming for years.

In some states the public wanted a tough crime policy but did not want to pay the costs that went with it. In Michigan, for example, the prison population soared in the 1970s as judges, reflecting public outrage about rising crime rates, imposed longer sentences. The legislature responded to public sentiment with laws setting stiff mandatory sentences. Taking advantage of Michigan voters' right to introduce legislation, a group concerned about the "coddling" of criminals pushed through a proposal that eliminated traditional good-time reductions in prison sentences. Then, in the 1980 election, that same public turned down a referendum proposition that provided for a tax increase to build new prisons.

The Michigan experience illustrates the fact that while the public is enormously concerned about crime, it is not usually excited by or even very much interested in figures demonstrating that prisons are overcrowded.

In fairness to the state of Michigan, it must be pointed out that the legislature exercised its right to override a popular referendum by a two-thirds vote. Good-time deductions from prison terms were restored, the legislature defending its action with two arguments: the effect rescinding those regulations would have on prison crowding and the position taken by prison officials that abolition of good-time sentence reductions would mean the loss of an important tool for controlling inmate behavior. Furthermore, the legislature went on to legislate a mandatory ninety-day reduction of sentences—thereby pushing up parole eligibility dates—whenever prison population exceeded capacity for more than thirty days.

Regardless of public indifference to prison overcrowding, sooner or later state and local governments find that, like it or not, they have to do something about their bulging prisons. Because of provisions in the Eighth and Fourteenth Amendments to the U.S. Constitution, both the federal and state governments are subject to the prohibition that "cruel and unusual punishments must not be inflicted." Those who defend the rights of prisoners constantly remind us that prison—prison itself—is punishment; an offender is not sent to prison to be punished there by inhumane treatment or conditions. And one has only to read descriptions of life in some overcrowded prisons to be aware that something "cruel and unusual" is happening.

In the 1970s and 1980s many prisoners, or groups working on behalf of prisoners, brought cases to the courts claiming that constitutional rights were being violated. Most of these cases were decided in the federal district courts; some reached the Supreme Court. Each decision was based on the facts of the particular case. The Supreme Court, for example,

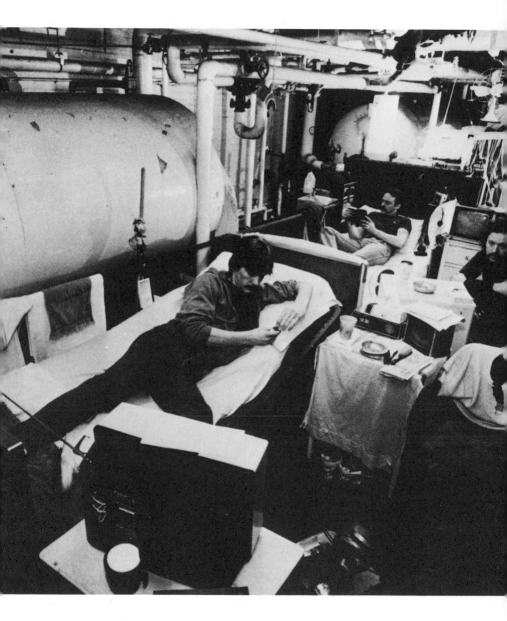

Because of overcrowding in a Dedham, Massachusetts, prison in 1983, some of the prisoners had to be housed in the boiler room.

laid down no broad principles to the effect that X square feet must be provided for each inmate or that only one inmate may be confined in a cell. But the Supreme Court, the lower federal courts, and the state courts have responded vigorously to the issue of prison conditions, worsened by overcrowding, and in 1984 at least thirty-eight states were under court orders to remedy crowded conditions in one or more of their prisons.

State and local governments given such court orders were confronted with other gloomy facts: The cost of building a maximum-security prison averages out to about $80,000 per inmate. And the construction costs involved in creating additional prison space are only the beginning; the cost of maintaining an offender in a state prison averages out to about $16,000 per year.

So former Attorney General William French Smith stated the obvious when he said, in March 1983, "We simply cannot afford to ignore alternative forms of punishment." His widely quoted statement reflected the consensus that has emerged among a substantial number of professionals in the criminal justice system: the conviction that prison space should be viewed as a *limited resource* and used accordingly, and that the move toward alterna tives to prison should be fostered.

True, Federal Bureau of Investigation statistics are beginning to show declining rates of crimes against property. True, the baby-boom generation will be well out of the high-crime-prone years by the 1990s. But rates of violent crime—murder, rape, and robbery, for example—have shown practically no change since 1980, and the prison population continues to rise each year. It appears that we will have to learn to use prison as a scarce resource and use alternatives to prison or we will have to spend such sums on prison construction that we ourselves will become, as has been observed, "victims of our war on crime."

The dollars-and-cents arguments for using alternatives to prison must be viewed from still another angle. When an offender is sentenced to prison and who, prior to arrest, had been working, paying taxes, and supporting a family, that sentence involves money costs to society beyond the cost of maintaining the offender in prison: he or she ceases to be a taxpayer and, more important, the family deprived of the earnings must often be supported by welfare.

But not just money is at stake here. Experienced criminal justice professionals, knowledgeable public officials, as well as many criminologists make the following points. First, they urge recognition of the fact that putting more people in prison for longer terms is not a documented solution to the crime problem. They point to crime statistics for the fifty states which, they maintain, fail to support either of these popularly held notions:

- That the crime rate (number of serious crimes per 100,000 population) will go down if the incarceration rate (number incarcerated per 100,000 population) goes up
- That the crime rate will go down if the lengths of prison sentences are increased

Minnesota and North Carolina, for example, have very similar crime rates, but North Carolina's incarceration rate is over five times that of Minnesota. The median time served by offenders in prison ranges from a low of nine months in New Hampshire to a high of thirty-nine months in Hawaii, and there is no correlation at all between the time served and the crime rate.

Second, thousands of people are in prison who, from the point of view of protecting society, do not need to be there. A recent study of the crimes for which offenders are in prison found that only forty-seven percent of prisoners had committed crimes of violence—homicide, rape, robbery, and assault. These are the offenders who, it is generally agreed, definitely belong in prison. One-third were there for property offenses—larceny (unlawful taking of the property of another), fraud, car theft, and burglary. These offenders, many believe, could be punished in ways other than incarceration. The remaining 20 percent were in prison for offenses grouped under the category "crimes against the public order," such as drug offenses. No generalization about the appropriateness of prison for these offenders can be ventured, because drug offenses vary so enormously.

It must be pointed out that there are sharp differences of opinion on the issue of the percentage of offenders in prison who really belong there. Those who define crimes of violence more broadly than the definition given above would classify a higher percentage of imprisoned offenders as people who belong in prison. Those who start with the assumption that all repeat offenders, regardless of their crimes, belong in prison, will come up with a still higher percentage of offenders who belong in prison.

Finally, those who argue for the use of alternatives to prison emphasize the broad professional and political consensus on the proposition that recidivism (relapse into crime by a convicted criminal) is far too high all over the United States. That is, an unacceptably high percentage of offenders, after serving one prison term, go back into the community, commit new crimes, and return—are recidivists—to prison. About 30 percent of offenders on parole, for example, return to prison for new crimes during the parole period.

Actually, alternatives to prison have been around for years: Probation and parole have long been accepted institutions in the criminal justice system. But, in the way in which they have been traditionally used, no one viewed them as solutions to the 1970s' problem of rising prison populations. Rather, there developed in those years, and there continues today, a groundswell of interest in making *more creative use of the existing alternatives* to prison and in developing *new alternatives.*

And things are happening along these directions. Federal and state legislation have explicitly legitimized the use of alternative kinds of punishments. The media are paying attention to innovative sentences. A number of organizations have appeared in the criminal justice world that specialize in drawing up alternative-to-prison sentencing plans, at attorneys' or courts' requests, for judges' consideration.

In 1979 the American Bar Association took the position that a judge, in deciding what sentence to impose upon a convicted offender, should consider a sequence of possible penalties. The judge should choose the first option that adequately protects the interests of society while contributing to the rehabilitation of the offender. The association's suggested sequence of options was as follows: probation, fine, restitution order, forfeiture, community service or supervision, intermittent incarceration, term imprisonment in an institution other than a confinement institution, and imprisonment in a confinement institution. In other words, the American Bar Association was saying to judges, "Think along eight or nine other lines before you think prison."

The following chapters explain the options listed by the American Bar Associatoin and describe some of the alternative-to-prison programs that are now in place here and there in the United States and being used to a limited degree by judges. However, these descriptions must be prefaced by three points that apply to any alternative-to-prison program or proposal.

The American Bar Association is a very prestigious organization but the mere fact that it recommends prison as a last resort and the fact that other distinguished groups have taken similar positions do not mean that alternative-to-prison programs are universally popular. The strong climate of opinion in their favor is locked in uneasy coexistence with a formidable "put criminals behind bars" advocacy, with a widely held conviction that only prison is punishment. Every proponent of prison alternatives emphasizes the absolute necessity to build a favorable climate of opinion before introducing any alternative program. Public and media support must be cultivated. Above all, the participants in the criminal justice process must be favorably disposed toward the program. If they are not, the program may exist but simply will not be used.

Second, persons committed to developing alternatives to incarceration are virtually unanimous in their emphasis that alternative-to-prison programs truly be *alternatives*. They urge that offenders should be placed in alternative programs only if, had these programs not been available, the offenders would have gone to jail or prison. They do not want the low-risk, minor-crime, first offender to be given a punishment—even assignment to an alternative-to-prison treatment or supervision program—if in the absence of that program he would have, in street parlance, "walked," that is, have been given a warning or suspended sentence. To use the phrase that appears over and over in the discussion of alternatives to incarceration, they most emphatically do not want to "widen the net of social control."

Finally, can we move on to the program descriptions with the heartening assurance that they will be a series of success stories? Not really. The descriptions will document that alternative-to-prison programs can make good things happen. They can make adequate provision for the public's security. They seem to have greater potential to rehabilitate offenders, to give more attention to victims' concerns, and to make positive contributions to community life. They seem to be less costly than incarceration. But an evaluation of alternatives to prison that meets modern research standards has not been carried out for many programs. The numbers simply are not there to warrant saying, "When Alternative Program X is utilized, recidivism drops by Y percent; if Alternative A is introduced, the jail population will drop by B percent."

The prevailing consensus, however, in the criminal justice field, seems to be that reliable evidence on the impact of alternative programs upon recidivism and the prison population should be sought. The absence of such data should not inhibit the search for and use of alternatives to incarceration. Given the woeful failure record of prison confinement, there is hardly any direction to go but up.

CHAPTER FOUR

THE NEW LOOK OF PROBATION—I NEW WAYS IN SURVEILLANCE

Probation was invented in 1841, almost by accident. John Augustus, a prosperous bootmaker, was in the Boston Police Court on a routine business matter. Augustus was an ardent advocate of the temperance (antidrinking) movement of that era, so when he crossed the path of a derelict brought into court as a "common drunkard," he felt impelled to talk with the man. They talked for just a matter of minutes, but long enough to convince Augustus that here was someone he could save. The judge listened in amazement as Augustus urged that the drunkard be released into his care, and then agreed to the experiment. Three weeks later a man changed beyond recognition stood at John Augustus's side in the courtroom, the first successful probationer.

That year Augustus assumed the responsibility for seventeen more alcoholics and then widened his range to other minor offenders. By the time he died, in 1859, just under 2,000 offenders had been given into his charge and only 10 had slipped away and become the first probation failures.

Today probation is part of the criminal justice system of all the states and of the federal government as well. In the opinion of many knowledgeable people, it is the most enlightened approach to the handling of offenders that has yet been devised. Two-thirds of all convicted offenders are sentenced to probation.

Basically, probation is a condition of controlled freedom. The offender is free in that he or she lives in a place of his or her own choice and maintains normal family, social, and employment ties. The offender is controlled by remaining under the jurisdiction of the sentencing judge and is subject to supervision of a probation agency.

Probation is imposed in one of two ways. The offender can be sentenced to a certain number of years on probation or a judge can impose a sentence of incarceration, suspend that sentence, and then impose a period of probation instead. Although judges have wide discretion in sentencing to probation, a substantial majority of the states bar probation in murder and rape cases and some states restrict probation for repeat offenders.

As the forms shown on pages 51 and 52 suggest, the teeth in a probation sentence lies in the fact that, if the conditions of probation are violated, the offender can be brought into court for a revocation hearing. If probation is revoked, the suspended sentence of incarceration goes into effect or a new sentence of incarceration is imposed.

General "conditions of probation" are routinely imposed as part of a probation sentence. Depending upon the state, general conditions may include any combination of the following obligations and prohibitions. The obligations may require the proba-

Affidavit

VIOLATION OF PROBATION

Before me, ... , Judge of
the .... Court in and for
.... County, Tenn., personally
came .... , who, being first duly
(Supervisor)

sworn, says that.............................. , hereinafter
(Probationer)

referred to as the aforesaid, was on the ....day
of.............................. , A.D. 19.... convicted of the
offense of..
in the .... Court of.................. County,
which Court suspended the imposition of sentence and placed the aforesaid on probation for a
term of .... ,
in accordance with the provisions of Title 40,
Chapter 29, of the Tennessee Code Annotated.

Deponent further states that the aforesaid has
not properly conducted h...self, but has violated
the conditions of h... probation in a material
respect by

....
(Supervisor)

Sworn to and subscribed before me
this .... day of ...., A.D. 19....

....
Judge of the .... Court
in and for .... County.

Warrant

In the Name of the State of Tennessee, to All and Singular the Sheriffs and Constables of the State of Tennessee:

WHEREAS,...has this day made oath before................................... that on the .... day of .... A.D. 19...., one ...., hereinafter referred to as the aforesaid, was convicted of the offense of ....in the ....Court of ....County, which Court suspended the imposition of sentence and placed the aforesaid on probation for a term of........................... in accordance with the provisions of Title 40, Chapter 29, of the Tennessee Code Annotated and that the aforesaid has not properly conducted h...self, but has violated the conditions of h... probation in a material respect by

THESE ARE, THEREFORE, to command you to arrest instanter the aforesaid ...., and bring h... before me to be dealt with according to law. Given under my hand and seal this .... day of .... , A.D. 19....

....

Judge of the ....Court
in and for ....County.

tioner to (1) be gainfully employed or attend school, (2) support dependents, (3) remain within the jurisdiction of the court unless given permission to leave, (4) cooperate with probation officers by responding to questions, and (5) pay a fee that covers part of the supervision costs. The prohibitions may direct the offender not to (1) violate any law, (2) associate with any known felon, (3) abuse drugs or alcohol, and (4) possess any firearm.

Beyond all this, special conditions may be imposed that are related to an offender's known special problems or to the nature of the offense. An offender with a history of emotional problems may be required to undergo therapy at a mental health clinic. A narcotics offender may be required to accept searches of his or her person, dwelling place, and car or other vehicle and accept unannounced tests such as urinalysis. Alcoholics are often required to participate in treatment programs. If the crime was connected with gambling, the offender will probably be forbidden to gamble. If the crime was assault involving a victim known to the offender, contact with that person may be forbidden.

Who enforces all the general and special conditions associated with probation? Systems vary: In some states the supervision of offenders on probation is handled by officers under the supervision of the courts; in other states it is handled by the Department of Corrections, that is, the agency responsible for running the prisons. The system most generally used, however, delegates the supervision of offenders on probation, and of those on parole as well, to a separate agency.

A more important question is: How does probation rate when judged against the purposes of punishment? Some probationers do fail and do commit new crimes while on probation. Society suffers from these crimes. And since inmates confined to prison cannot commit new crimes (except against each other), prison is obviously a better punishment than probation judged solely on the criterion of incapacitation. But there is another basis for judgment. What percentage of offenders, after completing their probation terms, commit new crimes? In other words, how effective is probation in rehabilitating offenders?

Studies related to this question have been made over the years and produced two fairly firm conclusions. A comparison of one hundred first offenders coming out of probation with one hundred first offenders coming out of incarceration yields significantly better results for probation. The recidivism rate for probatoners is clearly lower. Second, the overall rate of recidivism among offenders released from probation has been somewhat lower than that among offenders released from incarceration. These two findings constitute no glowing endorsement for traditional probation, however, because offenders given this sentence have usually been those considered better risks than offenders sentenced to incarceration.

As a matter of fact, traditional probation has been widely criticized over the years. In far too many places probation is looked upon as no sentence at all, as "getting off," rather than being punished. Case loads that make real interaction with clients impossible and inadequately trained probation officers are some of the reasons for lack of confidence in probation as an effective type of punishment. Many judges, with traditional probation or incarceration their only sentencing options, have expressed concern over the fact that they had to choose between a prison term that would be destructive for an offender and a probation placement that would neither help the offender significantly nor protect society adequately. It is not surprising, therefore, that some of the pioneering work in the field of prison alternatives focused on efforts to strengthen traditional probation and increase its effectiveness.

New methods in the surveillance of probationers have been introduced in some states, and their potential for reducing probation failure and recidivism after probation seems highly promising. The Georgia Intensive Probation Supervision program (IPS) is considered the strictest of the programs that have been undertaken in a number of states—New Jersey, New York, Texas, and Washington among them—to make probation a more effective punishment. Under the Georgia program each team of two officers is responsible for no more than twenty-five probationers, a case load that makes possible at least five contacts, and often more, each week. Each client has a curfew and the supervisors enforce it vigorously. Those who think a curfew check at eight o'clock means they can then go out on the town have not yet learned that a second curfew check at eleven o'clock is a distinct possibility. Georgia's IPS probationers are either employed or in school and, in addition, must fulfill community service and restitution orders.

Three other features of the Georgia program have demonstrated their usefulness. First, local police officers are notified of IPS participants in their area to foster cooperation between the police and county probation staff. Second, volunteers from the community serve as sponsors for IPS clients. Perhaps most appealing from a public relations standpoint,

IPS clients pay a probation fee of $10 to $50 per month, which covers part of the cost of their supervision.

Intensive supervision is, of course, more costly than regular probation, but far below the cost of maintaining an offender in prison. The Georgia figures, for example, are $0.75 per day for an offender on regular probation, $4.75 per day per offender in IPS, and $24.61 per day per offender in prison.

Does IPS really supply an alternative punishment for offenders who would have gone to prison had the program not been available? To make sure that IPS does do just that, most Georgia counties select their participants from among offenders who have actually been sentenced to prison but not yet started their terms. The sentencing judge must agree to the change in an offender's sentence from prison to probation, and the offender has the option of refusing IPS if desired.

In New Jersey IPS is most assuredly an alternative to prison, for offenders can apply for participation in the program only after having served thirty (but no more than sixty) days of their prison term. To be considered for the program applicants must submit a specific personal plan setting the goals toward which they will work while in the program. They must each have a community sponsor who is willing to assume responsibility for their behavior and must name a network team of people who agree to work with them on various aspects of the personal plan. An applicant who is accepted by both an IPS screening board and a three-judge resentencing panel must then successfully complete two ninety-day trial release periods; only after all that is the offender officially resentenced and officially part of the IPS program.

Those New Jersey offenders who are accepted for the IPS program are more than usually motivated to be successful on probation. They have had a taste of prison, the prison that awaits them if they violate their probation conditions. Some states that do not have IPS programs deliberately try to create this motivating effect by using an approach called a "split sentence" or "shock probation." Under this approach the judge retains jurisdiction over an imprisoned offender for a period of months and can order the offender's release to probation whenever, during this interval, such transfer is deemed appropriate. The shock of prison is intended to insure the success of probation.

Advocates of alternatives to prison point out that if judges use shock probation as a means of early release for offenders who would normally have drawn a significant term of incarceration, it is a genuine alternative. If, however, judges use it to incarcerate, even briefly, offenders who would otherwise have simply been sentenced to probation, it is an example of "widening the net of social control," which these advocates strongly oppose.

Some judges are beginning to use still another sentence option in combination with probation. They avoid the actual incarceration associated with shock probation but set as a probation condition the requirement that some part of the probation period be spent in a controlled residence. The facilities that are used as controlled residences are described in Chapter 8, on community corrections.

Does IPS work? One study of IPS involving about 1,500 New York State probationers produced encouraging findings. Although these were high-risk cases, the results showed that a substantially lower than normal percentage "skipped." The 40 percent who were judged ready for normal probation at the end of one year continued to be successful under less rigorous supervision; 95 percent of them kept out of trouble. Using these numbers as selling points, state probation officials met with judges around the state to spread the word. Probation officers were urged to recommend probation in their presentence reports; prosecutors and defense attorneys were informed so they could use the findings in plea bargaining.

The impulse to spread the word of IPS's success came from another finding of the study: When the IPS probationers were compared with imprisoned offenders, many inmates were identified who were so like the probationers that it would be fair to assume that they too would have succeeded had they been given the probation break. New York corrections people say, just as the national prison population survey showed, that one-third of their prison population is incarcerated for nonviolent offenses. Maintaining them in prison, they add, costs about $100 million per year. This is something to think about, advocates point out, if IPS could handle these offenders without threatening public security.

A probation officer who moves from an old-style, traditional probation program, with its high case loads, to an IPS program finds it to be a drastic change. To help with the transition, IPS officers always undergo a training program and, once in the new system, their reactions are very positive. Many seem to take an entirely new view of their role. The IPS officer is out in the streets more, where clients can be seen, as one says, "on their own turf."

One veteran IPS officer put it this way: "You can really get into people's problems and try to help."

He gives the example of Kenny, the child beater, who wanted a loan from his company credit union to buy Christmas presents for his family. Because he was already trying to pay off a high-interest finance company loan, the credit union turned him down. There had to be some way to get that finance company off his back, the story continues, so, "I asked him if he could work another shift. He jumped at it, and we found him a part-time, holiday-season job. We're so involved," he concluded, "it's enjoyable."

Few states would or could devote sufficient resources to probation to provide intensive supervision for all its probationed offenders. Nor is this deemed essential. It is usual to handle some probationers differently from others, and the increasingly sophisticated methods of classifying probationers that are now used are a second major way in which probation is being strengthened.

To illustrate this, meet Irwin Novice, who at the outset of his probation term was described like this: has full-time work; has had no prior arrests or convictions in the past year; shows no evidence of a drug or alcohol problem or other special problem; has stable family and social ties; has shown no aggressive behavior in the past year; shows good understanding of himself. Granted, Irwin is no typical criminal. But John, the bank officer who stole $30 million, probably would fit much of that description, as would many other white-collar offenders who commit property crimes. Irwin, John, and their ilk would, in a modern classification system, be placed in the "minimum supervision" category. They might be part of a case load of 200 to 300, and their only contact with their probation officer might be a monthly letter or telephone call to ensure that they are meeting the conditions of their probation.

Using the criteria suggested by the description of Irwin—employment, family and social relationships, criminal history, drug and alcohol use, general pattern of behavior, self-awareness—offenders with problems and disabilities can be identified and classified as needing "medium" or "maximum" levels of supervision. Different case loads and different officer–client contact requirements are set for each category.

The "right" size of case loads is an open question. There is no consensus among professionals on what a probation case load should be, although a range of thirty-five to fifty is often put forward. The American Correctional Association has set as a standard no specific client/officer ratio, merely the requirement that a probation officer "maintain personal contact with the offender." On this point, however, there is complete agreement: When the client/officer ratio gets "too high," probation is virtually worthless; and many probation systems in the United States are, or were, at that point.

Innovation related to probation has not been limited to changes in patterns of surveillance. The sentences that are being enforced by probation officers often reflect a more individualized and creative approach to the use of probation. Probation nowadays is often the framework of control within which a sentencing package of penalties and rehabilitation plans is imposed. Orders to perform community service and/or orders to make restitution are so important and so frequently imposed that they are described in detail in later chapters.

As mentioned earlier, defense attorneys can obtain a specific proposed sentencing package for an offender from organizations in the business of preparing them, such as the National Center on Institutions and Alternatives. Defense attorneys can offer sentencing packages of their own for judges' consideration and are being increasingly urged to do so.

The following are some examples that illustrate the creative and individualized approach that is being built into sentences within a probation framework:

In Texas a DWI (driving while intoxicated) offender can be sent to prison for two years or be fined $500 and placed on probation. One judge added this condition for some offenders: The offender's car must carry a bumper sticker that says, "The owner of this vehicle is on probation in the County Court of Law of Fort Bend County, Tex-

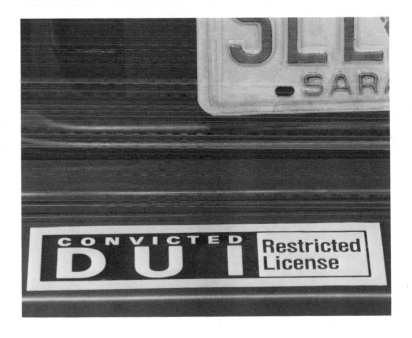

In Sarasota, Florida, first-time offenders convicted of driving while intoxicated display a bumper sticker on their cars: CONVICTED DUI *("driving under the influence").*

as, for driving while intoxicated. Report unsafe driving to Adult Probation Department, Richmond, Texas.''

The offense for which Kenny was convicted was that of beating his daughter with an electric cord. The child was removed to a foster home and Kenny was placed on probation. A special condition attached to his probation was that he and his wife attend Parents' Anonymous meetings and training courses.

Marie, the offender who bought furniture with rubber checks, was required under a special probation condition to attend financial counseling sessions.

James and Isabel knew their daughter was dying but did not take her to a doctor because they believed in faith healing. She died at age fifteen. James was convicted of reckless homicide and misdemeanor criminal recklessness and sentenced to five years in prison; Isabel was convicted on the criminal recklessness charge only and received a six-month sentence. Both sentences were suspended and the couple was placed on probation. A special condition of their probation was that their other two daughters be examined regularly thereafter by a licensed doctor.

Lillian killed the man she had been living with because, she claimed, she feared that he was going to kill her. Convicted on a guilty plea of second-degree manslaughter, she was sentenced to five years of probation. In addition to a heavy community service order, her special probation conditions were that she undergo vocational training and receive psychiatric help.

When Raymond killed his father, the circumstances were such that the judge himself remarked that the victim was a man ''the planet can rotate quite nicely without." Convicted of voluntary man-slaughter, Raymond was sentenced to five years' probation. Six months of psychiatric counseling was one special condition; the other was the require-ment that Raymond undergo training at a center for the preparation of missionaries and then spend two years in "Peace Corps-like" missionary work.

Jay ignored so many traffic summonses that his driver's license was suspended. He drove anyway and was picked up. Sentenced to probation for three months, his special condition was the require-ment that during that three-month period he spend nights and weekends at home. During the day he could leave home to go to work. "Jail moves into probationer's home" was the headline over the newspaper story of Jay's case, because Jay had agreed to a very unusual enforcement procedure. "Jail" was a black box that picked up radio signals emitted every thirty-five seconds from a transmitter strapped to Jay's leg. If the signals failed to send a continuous message during the hours he was sup-posed to be at home, a computer in the monitoring company's office would record the break and a checkup process would begin. If a violation of pro-bation were revealed, real jail loomed. "I hear that box kick in and I feel like tearing it from the wall," said Jay ruefully. "All this for driving with a sus-pended license." "All this" included a $410 fee to the private company that developed the device and monitors its users for the court.

Some probation professionals feel that the sur-veillance aspect of their work should predominate, that is, that their primary obligation is to keep an eye on their charges to ensure that they do not commit new crimes and that they do live up to the probation conditions imposed upon them. As one veteran officer put it, if a probationer has any

Jay Match, under three-month house confinement, works in his backyard. The three-ounce transmitter strapped to his leg above the ankle emits a radio signal every thirty-five seconds.

thought of committing a new crime, "we want him to know that we are right behind him." Obviously, keeping a watchful eye on persons who have broken the law is essential, for probation officers have a responsibility to society, but in the best modern programs, where effective surveillance is a top priority, meeting the needs of probationers is an equally top priority. Service delivery is heavily emphasized. To quote another veteran, "if a supervisor goes out with the attitude of trail 'em, nail 'em, and jail 'em, it's gonna ruin the whole program."

So the new face of probation, where it has appeared, includes new ways of meeting clients' needs, the subject of the next chapter.

CHAPTER FIVE

THE NEW LOOK OF PROBATION—II NEW WAYS IN SERVICE DELIVERY

I came across one of my probationers silently gazing at his newly acquired car, quite oblivious of all else and with the devotion young men normally reserve for members of the opposite sex. His second-hand vehicle looked to me like any other of similar age and design. He explained that what he was seeing was the car as it would be when he had finished working on it. I realized that the car was a projection of his own personality and that I could probably help him most effectively by working with him on the vehicle.

A probation officer

John Augustus would have rejoiced at the sensitivity to needs revealed in that excerpt from a probation officer's report; he would have endorsed the insight that the approach to a client must be unique to that client.

No questionnaire can substitute for a discerning eye and an understanding heart, but today's probation officer deals with numbers and time limits. An assessment instrument that helps the officer obtain a profile of a client early in their relationship unquestionably has its place.

The "Needs Survey," developed by the Missouri Division of Probation & Parole, is presented, in sharply abbreviated form, on pages 113–119. All the questions are there, but answer choices are given for only those questions that might not readily suggest to the reader a range of alternative responses. A careful reading of the survey will make very clear the aspects of probationers' lives that experience has shown must be the focus of probation efforts.

An excellent presentence report might well give a probation officer practically all the information about a new client that the survey reveals, but the advantage of having the client think through his or her situation, problems, and expectations is obvious. Furthermore, few clients enter probation accompanied by excellent presentence reports; many have none.

Many professionals feel that a probation term should begin with—and a classification of probationers should emerge from—a formal intake process in which needs are assessed, in which clients voice the kind and level of help they feel they need, and officers explain the help that will be available and the controls that will be imposed. An end product of such an intake process could be a probation contract between client and supervisor that specifically spells out a realistic answer to the question: What shall we work on first?

One characteristic of a modern probation system's ways of delivering services to its clients results from the changed relationship of the probation officers to the community in which they serve. Much more than in the past, they are involved with community people and community agencies; they use the community's resources; they move from the role of the one-on-one case worker to that of a broker of services. In delivering probation service, they start from the base of their clients' needs, their deficits in general education, vocational training, work experience, and the skills of ordinary daily living; they start from their clients' family situations, their employment situation, and their medical, emotional, alcohol, and drug problems.

The probation officers need to know the following: Who can offer what in vocational training? Who does tutoring? Where can psychiatric help and medical care be found? Who offers drug and alcohol programs? Who can help with housing? Who helps clients find jobs? Who makes jobs? Is anybody running a program like Vera Institute's Wildcat Service Corporation, which employs people without education, training, or experience, organizes them into work crews, and sends them out to fulfill clean-up, conservation, and messenger service contracts? What programs are available in the community's churches, through the Salvation Army, and the Volunteers of America?

The more the probation officers know, the better the job they can do. But, to repeat, experts emphasize that if the probation officers are to deliver adequate service, they must become brokers who bring clients and agencies together.

A second characteristic of modern probation service delivery is the use of volunteers. Many seem to be deeply involved with the probationers and are not just helpers in probation offices. "Our volunteers serve," reports one program, "by getting to know and becoming a helpful friend to one person on probation." Volunteers who are themselves arrested alcoholics help with alcoholism programs; others with relevant expertise work with clients whose problems range from drug abuse to emotional disturbance to mental retardation. Volunteers tutor; they conduct group intake sessions; they develop job contacts; they run workshops on how to hold a job successfully. Volunteers provide transportation for clients to and from job interviews and medical appointments and transportation for clients in search of housing.

While not a probation-related service, the following volunteer enterprise sounded too productive to omit: a course called "A New You," given by volunteers in the Kentucky Correctional Institute for Women. Its twelve weekly sessions cover a wide range of topics designed to build confidence and "improve the inner and outer person." It is all there: posture, poise, personal hygiene, birth control, and makeup techniques, plus attitudes, motivation, success principles, values, personality and manners, and goals. Completion of the course earns a certificate and a gift of cosmetics, and, it has been reported, some new persons do begin to emerge.

A third characteristic of modern probation service delivery is the planning of group programs to serve clients with common needs. The Suffolk County Probation Department in New York State, for example, has an alcohol treatment program that has demonstrated its effectiveness in reducing DWI recidivism. The DWI offenders are grouped into special probation case loads whose supervisors can focus on the alcoholism of their clients while carrying on field supervision. Andy Alcoholic knows there is no point in telling his supervisor, "I haven't had a drink today," unless it is true; the probation officer is probably carrying a portable Alco-Sensor that will tell all. The eighteen-week group counseling program for DWI probationers is unique in that the probation officer and the alcoholism counselor conduct the group as a team. Counselor and probation officer do not exchange memos about Andy Alcoholic; they are both in the room with him, for eighteen intensive sessions.

Kentucky's Bureau of Corrections operates a program of clearinghouses in its major metropolitan areas. Originally the program was planned as a job development and placement effort, but it soon became apparent that other services were essential if clearinghouse clients were to be ready to take the jobs that were available. So prevocational and on-the-job training have since been provided. In addition, a "living skills" program is now offered by the clearinghouse staff. Here the participants explore the process of communicating and interacting with other people, the process of decision making, and the process of problem solving. They learn to cope with such nitty-gritty matters as preparing résumés, filling out job applications, interviewing for a job, balancing a checkbook, reading a bus schedule, making a budget, and using credit.

Another area of clearinghouse effort is general education and development. Within the clearinghouse itself instruction is available from the basic reading level to preparation for a high school equivalency diploma. Also handled through the clearinghouse are contacts with community agencies for housing and medical and other services.

The persistence of shoplifting and its awesome costliness to business have spawned a number of programs. Designed for first-offense shoplifters, they are likely to consist of one to several group sessions supplemented by individual counseling sessions. The purpose is to help offenders understand not only the social costs of shoplifting, but also what made them commit the offense and to realize the consequences of repeated offenses. The incentive may be offered that the participant who maintains a clean slate after completing the program will have the record of the first offense and conviction destroyed.

The last probation program to be described comes from London. It was founded by a group of Inner London probation officers—the officer quoted at the beginning of this chapter was one of them—who understood that when young men are barred from driving because of traffic offenses, disqualification is more than a penalty, it is a challenge. How could they be helped through it?

Working with the police and a number of major motor and oil companies, the Inner London probation agency created the Ilderton Motor Project. Young offenders, but over the age of sixteen, who have been placed on probation and barred from driving can spend evenings at a motor center where all the necessary equipment for car maintenance and repair is at hand and instructors are available. Here they can work on their own cars or, if they wish, take part in a more unusual experience: Working in teams, they take unwanted cars turned over to the center by the police and get them ready for "banger racing." Banger racing involves putting a bunch of cars in an enclosed driving area where, on signal, each driver starts lunging around the track, using his car to bang other cars out of commission. The last car that can crawl around the field is the winner.

For many of these young people the experience of purposeful group effort and joint decision making—the group must decide, for example, which team member drives the team car—may be a first.

The minor cuts and bruises the drivers experience in their enthusiastic banging of car against car is, we are assured, more than compensated for by the glory of being the driver and the teammates of that surviving vehicle.

One final comment: The amazing thing about descriptions of probation service delivery is the number of people one reads about who are reaching out, in such a variety of creative ways, to help people who need help. John Augustus really started something.

CHAPTER SIX

THE REPARATIVE
SENTENCES—I
COMMUNITY SERVICE

Most of the regulars at the Sunshine Senior Citizen Center had finished eating lunch. As three rather young-looking men started to leave their places among the group, Leonard Leader rose and tapped on his glass for attention. "I'm sure all of you know that three good friends of ours are leaving us today. We wouldn't want them to go without letting them know how much we appreciate what they've done for us. Every time we look at these walls you fellows painted we're going to remember you and thank you. So let's hear it for Al and Bernie and Joey." The applause of a rousing standing ovation was ringing in their ears as the smiling trio departed.

No television camera covered the scene, newsworthy though it was. Al, Bernie, and Joey were three convicted offenders being thanked by users of a nonprofit community center for work done in lieu of jail sentences; they were being applauded for their participation in a community service program.

The purpose of community service programs is to place convicted offenders in nonprofit or tax-supported agencies so they can fulfill court orders to perform a specified number of hours of community service. The title of this chapter suggests the philosophy behind this alternative to prison. The word *reparation* means payment for a wrong or injury done. A community service sentence is a reparative sentence because it involves just such a payment. The entire community, so the theory goes, suffers from crime, and the offender performing service for the community is making reparation, or restitution, to the community for the harm he or she has done.

As was indicated in Chapter 4, community service is often a condition of probation; judges are free to order it under the wide discretion they traditionally enjoy in handing down probation sentences. In some states the law specifically authorizes community service as a separate sentence, sometimes naming specific groups of offenders who may be given such sentences or naming the types of offenses for which it may not be used. In New York State, for example, community service may not be used as a sentence for felonies, but since most felonies are plea-bargained down to misdemeanors, it remains a very available option.

Many states also permit offenders to work off fines they are unable to pay by fulfilling community service orders. In some states offenders convicted of minor crimes that would normally go on court records can, by fulfilling a community service order, have the arrest and conviction removed from the books.

As emphasized in Chapter 3, one major task in introducing community service as an alternative to prison is winning acceptance for the program, persuading prosecutors and judges that community service can be a tough sentence, persuading the public to believe not only that community service is a real punishment but also that convicted offenders working in the community pose no threat to their safety. The following question almost invariably arises in the planning stage of a community service program: Will community agencies be willing to accept convicted offenders as volunteer workers? The answer from programs all over the country is heartening. Agencies initially hesitant become completely open after one or two successful placements. Although opposition might be expected from organized labor, this has not been a real obstacle, for the work that community service volunteers do is practically always work that would have remained undone for lack of funds. The Sunshine Senior Citizen Center, where Al, Bernie, and Joey worked, for example, was described with terms such as "filthy walls," "windows that had not been cleaned for several years," and "floors caked with dirt and wax." Furthermore, it is the universal practice of community service programs to ensure in their arrangements with cooperating agencies that paid workers are not displaced by offenders fulfilling their community service orders.

Running a community service program is a daunting enterprise. Someone must enlist agencies to serve as work sites, interview sentenced offenders, make placements, report on accomplishments and failures, make recommendations based on these accomplishments and failures, enlist public support for the program, and raise money if funding is erratic or uncertain. Then there is the endless paperwork. All kinds of documents must pass back and forth among the judge, the offender, the agency in which the offender performs his or her service, and the supervisor who checks whether the offender is indeed peforming the service.

A wide variety of patterns for handling these responsibilities has emerged. Sometimes community service assignments are handled by local probation personnel and sometimes they are handled by personnel connected with the court system. Often an arrangement is made with a volunteer or nonprofit social agency in the community under which it takes over responsibility from the time of sentencing to the point where completion of service is certified or the offender returned to the court for failure to complete the designated assignment.

The pattern for handling on-the-job supervision varies. When Chuck Carefree is assigned to thirty hours of work in a hospital, somebody has to keep a record of his arrival · and departure times, note whether he is doing what he is asked to do rather than goofing off, and note any unacceptable behavior on the job. The usual practice seems to be for the agency using the offender's service to exercise this supervisory function, but, as will be seen in the New York City Vera project, when difficult clients are involved, offenders who are unaccustomed to normal work patterns, the program provides direct, on-the-job supervision through its own staff.

Where does the money come from to fund the administration of a community service program? Sometimes no new funds are provided; personnel and office space may simply be diverted from other correctional or court programs. When a program is run by a private nonprofit agency, the needed funds may come from a variety of sources. Prisoner and Community Together (PACT) is one well-known private agency that manages a number of community service programs in different cities. It gets its funds from foundation and corporation gifts and from contracts with the corrections departments of its client cities.

The range of people who receive community sentence orders as sentences or probation conditions is extraordinary: from the totally unskilled to highly trained professionals; from the totally anonymous (like our trio of painters) to the famous, like Mark Gastineau, the New York Jets' defensive end. Over a fifteen-week period Mark Gastineau taught football skills to young jail inmates to fulfill a ninety-hour community service order resulting from a conviction for assault. The range of service that volunteers are called upon to perform is equally remarkable. Cleanup tasks are repeatedly reported in descriptions of community service programs, as is work done in parks, on roads and in public buildings. But then there are the infinitely varied other services.

A young mother convicted of shoplifting, badly needed in her home by a sick child, knitted sweaters for a community agency. A graphic artist designed a brochure for the community service program handling his case; a model-plane hobbyist coordinated a model plane air show in a park; a bricklayer built an extension to the community firehouse; officials of a railroad corporation, convicted on illegal rate charges, lectured at two universities in subject areas in which they were expert.

The woman preparing a mailing to solicit funds for cancer research, the young girl helping in a Head Start center, the athlete guiding contestants in a Special Olympics track meet, the boy shelving

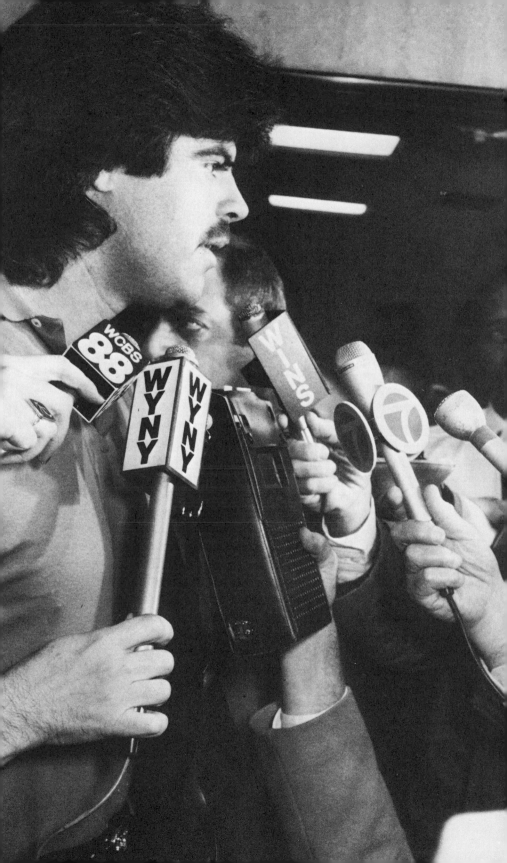

books in a public library, the telephone caller enlisting volunteers for the March of Dimes—any one of these, in a community where a community service program is in place, could be a convicted offender meeting the requirements of a community service order.

As part of the sentence package for a serious crime, a sentence involving community service can assume impressive dimensions. For example, Lee, vice-president of a construction company, was sentenced for the white-collar crime of bid-rigging on a highway construction project. His sentence prescribed that after seven days in jail he was to live and work weekends in a home for abused and neglected teenage boys in Nebraska, twenty-four hours a week for twenty weeks and then fifteen hours a week for three months. As a result, in the space of eight months, the home acquired a woodworking shop, equipped with funds Lee had paid as fines, a calf pen for a dairy calf project, a horse stall, and a large redwood deck, all top quality. While staying at the home, Lee took his turn at cooking, dishwashing, and cleaning and paid for his room and board.

When New York Jets star Mark Gastineau was convicted of assaulting a man during a brawl, he was sentenced to fifteen weeks of community service— teaching football skills to young prison inmates on Rikers Island, New York.

A court order of community service usually states the number of hours of service to be performed and the time period within which the sentence must be completed. It is usually possible to extend a deadline if, in the court's judgment, circumstances warrant the extension. Longer sentences for serious offenses are usually phrased not in terms of total hours but, as in Lee's case, as a number of hours of service a week to be performed for a specified period of months or years. The court order Harvey received provides another example of an order so phrased: In lieu of a possible fifteen-year prison term, Harvey was ordered, as part of his sentence, to perform fifteen to twenty hours of community service per week for three years.

Needless to say, a community service order does not relieve the convicted offender who is employed or going to school from the obligation of maintaining his employment or education. He must complete the assigned service in the evenings and on weekends.

In determining how much time should be allowed for fulfillment of a community service order, one program follows the formula that an employed person can complete twenty hours of service in a month without undue hardship. If this is a reasonable formula, it is clear that an order to perform fifteen to twenty hours of community service per *week* plus the requirement to maintain employment—and Harvey's sentence package was not unusual in requiring this—drastically affects the offender's life. It is not prison, but it is a tough sentence.

To help judges decide on the number of hours of service to assign in lieu of short jail sentences, formulas are sometimes given to avoid sentence disparity. Eight hours of community service for each jail day that would have been sentenced is one such formula.

In most of the examples of community service orders given above, it is clear that an effort was made to use the offenders' skills in their assignments. To make this kind of match and to arrange a time schedule and work site that are appropriate, the administrators of a community service program need information about their offenders. To get this information, one program uses the Offender Assignment Questionnaire, shown on pages 120–123.

The majority of those assigned to community service do only clerical or maintenance work, so one work site will do just as well as another, but some judges have very definite ideas on the kind of work they want an offender to do, in the sentence they designate not only the number of hours to be served but also the setting in which the service is to be performed. Some judges, for example, think the service assignment should be related to the offense rather than to the skills of the offender. Examples abound of judges specifying that a drunk driver spend his community service hours in the emergency room of a hospital.

Other judges and program directors feel that service related to the offender's skills or offense will not have the same impact as would be derived from service in a setting, and with people, with whom the offender is totally unfamiliar. The program director who placed Terence was certainly of that school of thought: Terence, a university senior arrested for indecent exposure—streaking at a bachelor party—spent forty-eight community service hours cleaning litter from the downtown streets of his university city. Forty-eight very sobering hours, no doubt, but they got off the record the conviction and jail term that would have been a serious threat to his law school candidacy.

Advocates of community service as an alternative to prison have been troubled by two criticisms that have been directed against it. Every expert who analyzes community service sentences has commented on the trend to use community service as an "add-on" penalty rather than as a genuine alternative to incarceration. Sometimes this happens because proponents of the community service alternative think that the best way to introduce it is the way that will seem least threatening to the community. So the traffic offender, or minor misdemeanant, whose case would previously have been dismissed with a warning is, under the new program, given a light community service sentence. All agree that if community service is to serve as a valid punishment option, it should be reserved for offenders who, by virtue of offense and record, would have been incarcerated. Otherwise its use is "widening the net of social control," which, as has been pointed out before, is no solution to any corrections problem.

Probably more serious is the charge that community service sentencing has been used primarily for white, middle-class first offenders, while poor, minority offenders have still been going to jail. Fortunately, convincing evidence is available that if this has been true, it need not be. In 1979 the Vera Institute of New York City set out to determine, by means of a pilot project, whether community service sentences could be used on a continuing basis for the kind of offender the institute described as "most likely to be sentenced to a short jail term— the unskilled, unemployed, minority offender who is convicted of a relatively minor charge (property misdeameanor) but who has a prior record of con-

Richard Wade, left, instructs Tyrone Israel at
the Dade County stockade. A criminal court
judge gave Wade the option of going to jail or
teaching reading and writing to prisoners once
a week. Wade accepted the teaching offer.

viction and multiple social problems." To document how significant it would be if community service could be used for offenders like these, Vera Institute pointed out that each year, in New York City alone, 8,000 jail sentences of ninety days or under are handed down by judges who feel that some punishment is needed and that probation is inappropriate.

Remember Peter, who stole plumbing fixtures, and Terry, who chose a decoy policeman as a robbery victim? Remember Al, Bernie, and Joey from the Sunshine Senior Citizen Center? They were part of Vera Institute's celebrated Bronx Pilot Project.

The Bronx Pilot Project staff knew from the beginning that if community service was to win acceptance by courts and public, it would first have to be recognized as enforceable, and offenders had to be the first to know that it was going to be enforced. The very first offender who received an assignment simply did not show up on the job site the first day. Project staff spent a weekend on the streets looking for him, finally tracking him down at his methadone treatment center. Streetwise to the prevailing lack of followup on summonses and suspended sentences, his surprised reaction was, "I never thought you'd come looking for me. I just didn't think it mattered."

To avoid complicated record keeping, the service sentence for all Pilot participants was set at seventy hours. Since they were all unemployed, they could work full days on their service assignments, which meant ten seven-hour days. Actually, most clients needed seventeen or eighteen days to complete their assignments, for time off had to be allowed for such personal business as welfare eligibility reviews and treatment center or clinic appointments. It was also recognized that staff at the work sites to which the participants were assigned could not offer the kind of supervision required by these offenders. Rules governing their conduct and performance at the job site were therefore very specific, as indicated by the agreement shown on the next page. Compliance with these rules had to be enforced for the best interests of the project, so Project staff carried out on-site supervision.

The last paragraph of the agreement promises the participants help in "understanding and obeying the conditions of my sentence," but supervisors soon found themselves giving more than that limited kind of help. The project did not want supervisors to become social workers, for that would limit the number who could be served in this *sentencing* enterprise, but when supervisors saw participants taking pleasure in the improvements their efforts were producing, when looking-ahead-to-something-positive attitudes surfaced in some participants, they were impelled to become involved.

Combine educational training deficiencies with little feeling of self-worth, little experience of goal-seeking behavior, and vivid memories of past failures, and it is easy to see why, on their own, even the participants who showed signs of wanting to turn their lives around would be unlikely to take advantage of training programs, seek out vocational counseling, and submit job applications. With these offenders it was usually not enough to say, "If you go to the XYZ Agency on Blank Street, they will tell you how to get into a woodworking program." All the preliminary calls and questions had to be handled by the Project staff so that the volunteer would have a specific person to see, a person who knew about his or her background and goals. Super-

NEW YORK COMMUNITY SERVICE SENTENCING PROGRAM

AGREEMENT   BOROUGH PROJECT_____

I, _____, have pled guilty to_____,
and as a condition of my sentence I agree to give service to my
community, as directed by the N.Y. Community Service Sentencing
Project.

1. I will give 70 hours of my time toward the improvement of
   the N.Y.C. community, by working at the jobs assigned to
   me by the Project. I will do this for seven hours each
   day for ten days, Monday through Friday, or until I have
   completed 70 hours.

2. Everyday, beginning with _____, I will come to the
   Project worksite by 9 o'clock a.m. and I will not leave
   until 5 o'clock p.m. I understand that the Project
   will provide me with $2.00 daily to buy lunch and $2.00
   daily for transportation to and from the community worksite.

3. I understand that I may be terminated from the Project
   and returned to the court for a new sentence:

   (a) if I arrive at the worksite late, or leave without
       permission ;

   (b) if I use physical violence toward anyone, or display
       any sort of weapon, on or around my worksite;

   (c) if I steal from the Project or from anyone on or
       around my worksite;

   (d) if I buy, sell or use drugs, marijuana, beer, liquor
       or wine on or around my worksite, or if I am high or
       drunk on my worksite;

   (e) if I deliberately destroy any tools or personal pro-
       perty of the Project or of other people at my work-
       site; or

   (f) if I am arrested on a new charge and detained.

I understand that if I must be late, or must leave early, or if
I must leave my worksite during the day, I can call the Project
Office (___)_____or speak with my Site Supervisor. I will not
be terminated from the Project as long as I have a valid and veri-
fiable reason for being late or absent and have received permission.

I understand that my obligation to the Court, to provide the
community with 70 hours of service, means that I will have to make
up any time I miss because I am late or absent on any of my ten
regular days. I will make up that time as the Project Director or
my Site Supervisor tells me to.

I understand that disobedience to my Site Supervisor, wrestling,
boxing, shouting, and bickering are not a service to the community;
if I engage in them on my worksite, it may lead to my termination
from the Project and my return to court for another sentence.

I understand that I may ask the Project Director, Support Service Coordinator or my Site Supervisor for help in understanding
and obeying the conditions of my sentence.

At sentencing, Judge _____ advised me that if I violate
the conditions set forth in this agreement I will be sentenced to
_____ (days/months) of imprisonment.

_____   _____
     Date   Signature of Project Participant

                              _____
                              Signature of Project Representative

visors became, like good probation officers, brokers of services. They contributed to success stories, and they also knew failures.

It is good to report that Vera Institute is still running a community service sentencing project for about a thousand Peters, Terrys, Als, Bernies, and Joeys each year, and not just in the Bronx, but in other boroughs of New York City as well.

Community service advocates cannot back up their arguments with numbers proving reduced recidivism or lower jail and prison populations. They can, however, cite repeated instances of job offers growing out of community service assignments and of volunteers staying on as volunteers after their community service orders were fulfilled. From communities all over the country, they can quote program directors who multiply hours of service performed under court orders by the hourly minimum wage and say, "Last year, this community received free, work worth $_____. Furthermore, this community saved the $_____ it would have cost to keep the _____ convicted offenders who performed that service in jail, had no alternative punishment been available."

CHAPTER SEVEN

THE REPARATIVE SENTENCES—II RESTITUTION

Hank has moved from Oldtown, where he grew up and where his father still lives, to Newtown. There he works during the day and goes to school at night. Every month he mails a check to a court office in Oldtown. The court, in turn, mails a check to Mack. Mack lives in Oldtown, right down the street from where Hank grew up. Mack is at home now, after surgery necessitated by gunshot wounds. He is recovering satisfactorily, but it will be a month or more before he can go back to work.

Hank is on probation, convicted of aggravated assault for shooting and seriously wounding Mack. His probation conditions required the move from Oldtown and the work/school way of life. The monthly checks meet his final probation condition: that he make restitution to Mack for medical expenses and lost wages.

Restitution to the victim of a crime is an alternative-to-prison punishment that is being used with increasing frequency. It is a modern penalty, yet its

A young first-time offender makes his weekly visit
to the courthouse payment window to pay back the
victim of his crime. He is participating in the
Quincy, Massachusetts, "Earn-It" program to make
restitution for the crime he committed, and he
must report to this window each week until the
damages have been completely repaid.

history goes back to centuries before prisons or probation were even thought of. This bit of law, from the oldest known civilization of the Middle East, is some 4,000 years old: "If a man has broken another man's bones, he shall pay (him) one mina of silver." Whether or not we know how much value, in today's terms, a mina places upon broken bones, the principle is clear: Restitution (payment for loss, damage, or injury) must be made for the broken bones—restitution to the *victim*.

With the founding of modern nations, some 500 or 600 years ago, came the idea that the important aspect of crime is that it is an offense against the *state*, that is, against all the people of the community. This idea is the accepted basis of the criminal justice system today, and the names by which criminal cases are identified reflect it. If Carl Criminal were brought to trial for robbing Victor Victim, the name of the case would be *The People v. Carl Criminal.*

For years the principle has been accepted that those who seek financial restitution for losses resulting from a crime or injuries sustained during a crime have no place in the criminal courts; they have had to seek restitution by bringing a suit in the civil courts, the courts concerned with settling private grievances and claims. This is changing. Today restitution by criminals to victims, or "symbolic restitution" to the community, is very much an idea whose time has come. Restitution is generally accepted as a legitimate way to make offenders pay for their crimes. In fact, a restitution order in a sentencing package may make that package acceptable to those who would deem it otherwise too soft. Restitution to victims is accepted as a sentencing option or probation condition in all the states and by the

federal government. Programs under which restitution to victims is arranged and monitored are in
force in many of the states.

Often restitution is the only special condition
attached to a probation sentence, and probation
officers working with groups of such offenders are
carrying out what amounts to probation/restitution
programs. The following details suggesting how restitution works in practice comes from one such program.

First, whenever possible, officers plan for victim
and offender to meet and decide upon the amount
of restitution to be exacted in money or services.
Because the officers feel that the victim should
have an opportunity to air his or her feelings about
what has happened, the first contact of the probation officer is with the victim alone. When the victim
expresses a willingness to meet with the offender,
the offender is so informed; the offender is not given
the option of refusing to meet his or her victim.
When the meeting takes place, the probation officer acts as a go-between in arriving at a restitution
figure. If the victim says the cost of replacing, say, a
stolen television set is $500 and the offender disa-
grees, the probation officer might send the offender to a television shop to get actual prices. Then the
officer works with the two parties until the restitution
penalty is agreed upon, a schedule of payments or
service arranged, and the court notified. From that
point on, normal probation supervision ensues, with
the officer checking that restitution payments are
made on schedule.

As noted earlier, in some places there are government or nonprofit agencies whose function is to
provide the machinery to investigate victims' losses,
prepare restitution payment plans, and monitor restitution orders for the courts. Take Donald's experi-

ence, for example. Donald broke into the Matz family's home and stole cash, a television set, and jewelry valued at several hundred dollars. In a face-to-face confrontation, Donald and the Matzes, with the aid of a representative of the local victim/offender reconciliation program, agreed upon a restitution plan. Under it Donald performed forty hours of yard work for the family.

Advocates of victim/offender confrontation in a restitution program maintain that this process allows offenders to get an idea of the trouble and pain they have caused and gives victims the chance to vent some of their feelings. One restitution program reports that, although many victims are unwilling to go through with the confrontation process, over half the victims with whom it deals are willing.

In at least two states, Georgia and Mississippi, a number of confinement centers have been established that exclusively accommodate offenders convicted of property crimes that would ordinarily be punished by prison terms. Instead of going to prison, the offenders live at the centers and go out to work. Their earnings are used to support their families, pay taxes, pay for room and board at the centers, pay any fines that were imposed in their sentences, pay clothing and medical expenses, *and* make payments against the amount of restitution awarded by court order to their victims.

In the Georgia Restitution/Diversion Program the offender remains in the center for four to six months and then goes home but remains on probation until his or her restitution commitment has been met. In both states the centers offer services beyond food and shelter—services such as counseling, education and training programs, and help with drug and alcohol problems. Programs like these are called residential restitution programs, because participants must live in a controlled facility for at least part of the time during which they are making restitution payments.

Alabama has a nonresidential program called Supervised Intensive Restitution (SIR), which does not divert convicted offenders from incarceration but, rather takes eligible offenders out of jail. No one doing time for a crime of violence, a sexual offense, child molestation, or a drug sale is considered for this program. To be eligible the offender must be at least eighteen, in good health, and must have a good behavior record in jail. The offender must also be able to produce a sponsor with whom to live, usually a member of his or her family, and who will formally accept the responsibility of supervision. A full forty-hour work week is required, and those unable to get jobs are assigned to community service.

The SIR program consists of three phases. In Phase I, which lasts three months, participants are very closely supervised. During each week there are at least four face-to-face contacts in the offender's home, at least two contacts at the work place, and another contact when the offender goes to the program office to pay the supervision fee that is a required obligation of the program. A ten o'clock curfew is strictly enforced. Successful completion of Phase I permits entry into the slightly less rigid nine-month Phase II, during which the number of face-to-face home contacts drops to two per week, one job contact per week becomes the minimum, and the curfew is changed to eleven o'clock. When entry into Phase III has been earned, the curfew may be dropped completely, and home visits and employment verification may be monthly events. As the name of the program suggests, SIR participants must fulfill court restitution orders in either payments to victims or community service.

While restitution often involves relatively small obligations—not small, of course, to the individuals who must meet them—it can assume substantial proportions. For example, Sally was sentenced to three years in prison for stealing $160,000 from the bank for which she had worked. The sentence was suspended for an alternative sentence package that combined over 700 hours of community service at a girls' home, with restitution of $100,000 to the bonding company that covered the bank's loss— $300 a month for about twenty-eight years. As another example, the court-accepted restitution plan in the case of E.F. Hutton & Company ran to millions of dollars.

Concerning this last case, and others, the observation must be made that a restitution penalty does not always satisfy everybody. In the E. F. Hutton case, for example, the crime involved was a complicated one, but basically it gave the company interest-free use of millions of dollars by writing the kind of checks that Marie wrote to buy her furniture and for which she was placed on probation. Critics objected that the fines imposed and the full restitution undertaken by the company to those who had been cheated by this swindle involved no criminal penalties for any of the individuals who knew about what was going on.

The father of the young man struck and killed by Henry, the drunk driver introduced in Chapter 1, was infuriated by the final sentence: Henry was placed on probation with three conditions: He had to hold his job, go to school at night until he obtained a high school diploma, become an affiliate of Alcoholics Anonymous, and—as symbolic restitution—give eight hours a week of service in a hospital emergency room. The father wanted vengeance.

While there are many reports of high rates of completion of restitution obligations, advocates are disturbed by two facts that have emerged from studies of this penalty. First, it was found that restitution is frequently an add-on penalty. In many instances, offenses that in the past drew probation only, or fines only, seem to be getting probation with a restitution condition, a fine, *and* a restitution order. Restitution is not an alternative to prison unless offenders who would have gone to prison are diverted from prison to fulfill restitution orders. Also disturbing is the finding that the victims who are receiving restitution are, in a majority of cases, businesses, governments, or organizations, rather than individuals.

Reservations aside, there is no question that the day of the victim is here, or at least rapidly arriving. Restitution by offenders is not the only development of recent years in the interests of victims. In addition to permitting or requiring victim impact statements in presentence reports, about twenty-five states now have laws providing for various degrees of participation by victims in the process of granting or denying parole. About forty-two states have compensation programs under which payments are made to victims for losses or injuries. New York State's Crime Victims Compensation Board, for example, pays out about $9 million per year. At least one state has passed a law under which victims can claim the profits that criminals make from books about their crimes.

A law has been introduced in one state under which, if it is passed, the government will be able to confiscate property belonging to a convicted felon up to an amount equal to that gained from the crime. Proceeds from the sale of that property will go to victims of the crime. The federal government has such a forfeiture penalty now, although the proceeds do not go to a victims' compensation fund. For example, a nine-bedroom oceanfront home in Miami was recently sold by a federal auctioneer for $919,000. The house, which was formerly owned by an offender serving a forty-year term for marijuana smuggling, was seized under a federal racketeering law. This law provides that an offender convicted of conspiring to commit a number of crimes can lose personal possessions—homes, cars, airplanes, boats—bought with the profits from those illegal enterprises. Many knowledgeable people in the criminal justice field advocate heavy economic penalties like these as weapons to fight white-collar and organized crime.

Because for many years the public has been impatient with what was perceived as more official concern for criminals than for victims, restitution is an attractive alternative-to-prison sentence and has a wide advocacy as an appropriate penalty for property crimes. The by-product restitution sometimes produces is certainly not central in criminal justice planning, but it has its own significance. Consider the following

When Donald completed his yard work for the family whose home he had burglarized, Mr. Matz's comment was simple but revealing: "As far as I'm concerned, I'm happy I know him."

CHAPTER EIGHT

COMMUNITY
CORRECTIONS—
THE UMBRELLA
GOAL

On July 4, 1985, the Reverend Sun Myung Moon, sur-
rounded by dozens of media people, left the federal medium-security prison that he had entered, with
equally heavy media attention, on July 20, 1984,
after a highly controversial conviction on an income
tax charge. His eighteen-month sentence having
been reduced by five months for earned "good
time," he had forty-six days yet to serve. He
reported that evening to Phoenix House, a residence run by a private, nonprofit agency. Except
for occasions when he was granted an overnight or
weekend pass, Reverend Moon had to be in Phoenix House by ten o'clock each evening. He was
allowed to leave the residence at seven o'clock
each morning and to carry on his church duties during the day. Reverend Moon served the last forty-six
days of his sentence in Phoenix House. Reverend
Moon figures in this book only because he is a real-
life example of a person emerging from a prison
term and entering a *community residential facility.*

The preceding chapters have focused on convicted offenders diverted from prison and living, under supervision, in places of their own choice. Two references have been made, however, to residential facilities that serve as places of confinement but which are not jails or prisons: the centers where participants in Georgia's Restitution/Diversion Program live and the "controlled residence" mentioned as a special condition imposed on some probationers. Such a controlled residence is usually a community residential facility like the one that housed Reverend Moon on his way out of prison, that is, a halfway house.

Halfway houses have not always held this kind of population mix. They acquired the designation "halfway" houses because the offenders in them were all *halfway out* of prison. In the last twenty years or so, halfway houses have been used increasingly by judges who do not want to impose incarceration but do want the offenders they are sentencing to be, for a while at least, in a *controlled* place of residence. The judge who sentenced Gerald, for example, on a conviction for embezzlement imposed a ten-year prison term and then suspended that sentence and ordered Gerald to live for three years in a halfway house and then complete a five-year term of probation.

Halfway houses are thus becoming places where some of the residents can be thought of as *halfway in* to prison. Michigan's recent expenditure of over a million dollars for community halfway houses demonstrates the increasing use of this kind of placement. These halfway houses are to be used for young felony offenders on probation for whom controlled residence is ordered.

On a par in importance with halfway houses are the community residential facilities known as prerelease centers or work/education release centers. In earlier days parole sent offenders directly from prison to their home community, and many simply could not successfuly make the sharp adjustment from prison to freedom. So prerelease programs were developed, furlough systems under which qualifying offenders are released before their earliest possible parole dates to work or pursue education or training in or near their local communities. They are confined during these furloughs to work release centers. Here, in a setting that is closer to normal life than that in a prison, it is hoped that offenders will develop, before release on parole, the skills and attitudes needed to function in the community. The goal of rehabilitation, in other words, is broadened to encompass the goal of reintegrating the offender into society.

There are also an amazing variety of specialized community residential facilities to accommodate convicted offenders with special problems, notably drug and alcohol abuse. California is one of the states that has a specialized prerelease residence for women with preschool-aged children. The day care available in the residence enables the women to hold their required jobs and still have their children live with them. Some of these specialized community residential facilities are operated by state or local government agencies; some are operated by private nonprofit agencies under contract to government agencies.

The term *community residential facility* should suggest an image very different from that evoked by *prison.* A smaller place, definitely: Some halfway houses accommodate as few as five residents, although the average runs to about twenty-five. And a different-looking place: While many community residential facilities were built for the purpose they serve, many are large, old houses or former school houses converted to their new use. An unfortunate exception to the nonprisonlike look of community residential facilities is the work release center housed in a section of a local jail. While it is conceded that any work release center is better than no work release center, this kind of housing for a center is generally deplored.

The purposes and programs of halfway houses and prerelease centers are basically alike, as are their counseling and other services. The residents of halfway houses, as pointed out earlier, may be probationers or prison inmates on their way out of prison for one reason or another. Parolees are sometimes accommodated there. All the residents of work release centers are furloughed prisoners. The centers tend to be larger, operated directly by government agencies, more structured in their rules and procedures, and more similar one to another. Hence life inside a work release center is easier to decribe than life in a halfway house. To convert the picture of life in a work release center to life in other community residential facilities, subtract from the description that follows the field supervision details and an internal restriction or two. The key characteristics are the same. First, the residents have a way of life that is a challenging mix of freedom and control. They are free to work or study in the community and make use of its facilities, but they are controlled in their comings and goings and in their movement within the community. Second, they live with the awareness that infractions of the rules or new crimes will send them forthwith to jail or prison.

The furloughed offender is not on his own when he walks out of the work release center to go to his or her job or school; being under supervision in the field is part of the custody aspect of a work release program. A minimum of one field contact per week is a typical level of supervision, but some furloughees may require a daily visit by a field supervisor to the job or school site.

A twofold purpose is involved here: For the offender who needs an incentive to stay on the job, the awareness that absence or poor performance is not acceptable may provide the support he or she needs. For the community, field contacts are evidence that offenders on work release are truly being monitored. This builds assurance that the presence of a center in the community is not a threat to community security.

Good field supervisors make every effort to be tactful and unobtrusive. Employers and school supervisors must know that the furloughee is being monitored; and the furloughee must be aware of being monitored, but both objectives are achieved by competent supervisors without singling out the furloughees in an embarrassing way.

It is usual for residents of work release centers to be permitted to use such community services as barbers and beauticians, libraries, and recreational facilities, but permission to make these community contacts must be cleared with the center staff beforehand.

In some programs short-term temporary release from the work center can be obtained for such specific purposes as family emergencies, job searches, and arranging for postrelease housing. In some programs an excellent record of behavior in a work release center can earn the additional taste of freedom offered by a weekend at home.

Centers are not so-called secure facilities: Residents go in and out to jobs and school, so the locks and fences that are in place are intended to control unauthorized entrance rather than to prevent escape. But there is no mistaking a center for anything but a correctional facility. Aside from tight check-in and check-out procedures, any number of controls remind the residents that they are in custody. The public address system may have two-way audio capability so that sounds from rooms and hallways can be picked up in control stations. Tools that could be used as weapons and cleaning supplies containing dangerous chemicals may be locked away.

Although strip searches are not characteristic of centers, pat-down searches of residents reentering the center may be random or routine. Rooms and personal property are subject to search. A head count, accompanied by a check on sign-out records, may be made at every staff shift change. Drug and alcohol use are absolutely forbidden and random urinalysis and breathalizer or intoxalyzer readings may be used to check for infractions.

Public means of transportation must, of course, be used by many residents. If the use of private cars must be permitted, careful checks on registration, insurance, and licensing are likely. Late returns from outside activities are rule infractions and anxious residents stuck in traffic or caught in train delays have been known to bring notes from policemen or conductors to document their reasons.

Good relations with the community in which a center is located are a crucial factor in its success. This is one reason why advocates of work release place such heavy emphasis on screening offenders who apply for the program. Repeated success stories of offenders smoothly reintegrated into normal life can expect no media attention. But the storm that will arise over an offense committed by a furloughed prisoner may threaten a work release program throughout a state. The success rate in these programs, incidentally, is high, with some studies showing that about 80 percent of the offenders who are given the work release opportunity complete it successfully.

The desire for good relations with the community also explains why center administrators are urged to arrange for residents' participation in volunteer services. The cleanup, repair, painting, landscaping, or other services the center's residents perform benefit the community and build a favorable image for the facility. Also, it is hoped, they give the residents a feeling of belonging to the community.

The term *community corrections* is sometimes used narrowly to refer only to correctional institutions sponsored and operated by local—city or county—units of government. Used in this sense, a county jail would be among the institutions that are categorized as community corrections. Used in a broader sense, as it is by many corrections profes sionals and as it is used in this chapter, *community corrections* includes any alternative-to-prison program that enables convicted offenders to maintain, under supervision, employment or education ties and family and social ties with the outside community. Under this definition, community residential facilities clearly are community corrections; so are probation, community service, and restitution programs, for all make it possible for community ties to be maintained. All are punishments and involve the control of the convicted offenders, but society is not burdened with the costs of maintaining them in prison and, perhaps, maintaining their families on welfare. Nor need the security of society be threatened.

Faced with a choice between trying community-based alternatives to prison and building more prisons, it is small wonder that many state governments are opting, at least partially, for the former. Many have subsidized programs like intensive probation to encourage local communities to try them. As described in this book, a number of states have planned, funded, built, and operated prerelease centers, restitution/diversion centers, halfway houses, and other alternative-to-prison facilities.

The most recent development on the alternative-to-prison front has been moves in state legislatures to foster local community corrections initiatives. Following the precedent set by Minnesota's Community Corrections Act of 1973, a number of states, including California, Colorado, Iowa, Kansas, Maryland, Ohio, Oregon, Vermont, and Virginia, have passed, under a variety of titles, legislation to encourage communities that wish to participate to develop correctional facilities, services, and programs at the local level.

These laws differ in their details but all involve the same basic approach. A participating community is rewarded by a financial subsidy when it retains nonviolent offenders in local programs instead of sentencing them to state prisons. Con-

An inmate, riding a new motorcycle he bought with his savings, waves as he leaves a Los Angeles correctional facility for his job 9 miles (14 km) away. He is participating in the County Probation Department's work furlough program. Under the program, prisoners who acquire outside employment may be absent from jail for up to twelve hours a day.

versely, a financial penalty may be incurred if non-violent offenders *are* sentenced to state prisons. A community that chooses to participate in one of these state programs usually must set up a formal corrections-planning process. It must name a local board on which all the parties involved in the criminal justice system are represented—judges, prosecutors, attorneys, corrections officers, and the general public—and give that board the power to make decisions on community corrections projects.

The emphasis on local planning and decision making reflects awareness that the totally centralized control of corrections efforts has its drawbacks. When a state decides to build a diversion center in Centerville, for example, a flurry of "not in my neighborhood" campaigns may erupt. A diversion facility planned and sponsored by representative leaders of Centerville, on the other hand, might be accepted as "our center."

Subsidies received under a community corrections act come with strings attached. Usually the money may not be used for construction; a community cannot simply elect to build more jails to keep more offenders in its own backyard. The money may not be used to fund programs already in place. If Upstate County has had a probation department for years, the state subsidy could not be used to pay the salaries of that department's personnel, but if Upstate County's planning board decides to start an intensive supervision unit in the probation department and divert serious but nonviolent offenders from state prison to that IPS program, this would constitute appropriate use of subsidy funds.

In short, a mechanism is now in place in at least several states through which more local governments will be able to do what the pioneering places described in this book are now doing. And, to advocates of alternatives to prison, this is encouraging.

This book must end, however, with words of caution. It would be unrealistic to ignore the fact that during the past ten years moves toward the use of prison alternatives have been outpaced by moves toward the expansion of prison capacity. The equation "more imprisonment equals less crime" remains for many an appealing "solution" to the "crime problem," despite challenging evidence to the contrary.

It will take all the patience, persistence, and courage that advocates of prison alternatives can muster and all the leadership they can enlist to weaken the appeal of that simplistic crime control slogan and broaden support for their clear and urgent message:

There are ways of punishing nonviolent criminals that are more humane, equally safe, and less costly than the ways we are using now, and we should try them instead of prison.

APPENDIX

NEEDS SURVEY

1. What is your marital status?
2. What is your sex?
3. What is your age?
4. Do you live in a halfway house? *(Halfway houses are described in Chapter 8.)*
5. Are you on probation or parole?
6. My level of education is ____ .
7. Are you a student?
8. In your opinion, what is the most important service your probation officer (PO) can provide for you? (Check one.)

____ (1) finding adequate housing
____ (2) finding a job
____ (3) helping you get more training or education
____ (4) finding help for your drug problem

_____(5) finding help for your drinking prob-
lem
_____(6) finding medical care assistance
_____(7) finding professional counseling ser-
vices for you and your family
_____(8) helping the community become ac-
cepting of people on probation
_____(9) giving some personal guidance

9. How do you think a probation officer should help a client like yourself find a job? *Choices reflect increasing levels of help.*
10. How do you think a probation and parole officer should help a client like yourself find adequate housing?
11. How do you think a probation officer should help a client like yourself receive educational training?
12. How do you think a probation officer should help a client like yourself receive counseling for your family?
13. How do you think a probation officer should work to make the community more accepting of people on probation and parole?
14. Have you had problems in finding a job because you are on probation or parole?
15. If yes, how much of a problem is it?

If you are EMPLOYED, answer questions 16 through 24. If you are UNEMPLOYED, begin at question 25.

16. What do you like about your job?
17. Are you looking for another job?

18. I am staying on my present job because . . .
19. Do you have problems with your employers?
20. Which one best describes your problems with your employer?
21. What is the biggest problem you have with your job? (Check one.)

_____(1) getting to work on time
_____(2) finding transportation
_____(3) I dislike what I am doing
_____(4) putting up with working conditions
_____(5) not getting injured or hurt
_____(6) work is boring
_____(7) don't like this type of work
_____(8) no problems

22. Which best describes your job? *Choices differentiate between full-time, part-time, and on call.*
23. Which best describes the time you work?
24. What is the hourly rate that best describes your situation?

If you are UNEMPLOYED, begin here.

---

25. Why did you leave your last job? (Choose only one.)

_____(1) to look for another job
_____(2) was fired
_____(3) was laid off
_____(4) the job was only temporary
_____(5) didn't like what I was doing

_____(6) couldn't work out transportation or other similar problems

26. How long were you employed on your last job?
27. How many jobs have you had in the past two years?
28. How long have you been unemployed?
29. Being unemployed has. . . . (Choose only one.)

_____(1) caused problems with family
_____(2) caused problems with friends
_____(3) got me into more trouble
_____(4) led me to give up looking for a job
_____(5) encouraged me to use drugs
_____(6) encouraged me to use alcohol
_____(7) caused me to feel useless and depressed
_____(8) caused me to lose interest in training for jobs I'm interested in
_____(9) caused no problems

30. In your opinion, why are you unemployed? (Choose only one.)

_____(1) no jobs available
_____(2) lack of skills
_____(3) I'm on probation or parole
_____(4) alcohol problem
_____(5) drug problem
_____(6) don't get along with other people
_____(7) no transportation
_____(8) I don't know
_____(9) other (specify)_____

31. What, for you, makes the best kind of job? (Choose only one.)

    ____(1) high salary
    ____(2) job is interesting
    ____(3) the hours and days are all right
    ____(4) good fringe benefits
    ____(5) I have friends who work there
    ____(6) there is chance for training
    ____(7) there is chance for advancement
    ____(8) working with people who like me
    ____(9) learning to do a skillful job
    ____(10) directing others
    ____(11) I don't know

32. In the past, which has given you the most trouble? *(Choice is between finding and keeping a job.)*

33. Which has given you trouble in finding a job? (Check as many as apply.)

    ____(1) no jobs you are skilled for
    ____(2) no jobs you are interested in
    ____(3) don't know where to look
    ____(4) talking with employers
    ____(5) transportation to look for a job
    ____(6) alcohol
    ____(7) drugs
    ____(8) I'm on probation or parole
    ____(9) I have had no trouble

34. Which has given you trouble in keeping a job?
35. What kind of skills do you have to bring to a job?
36. How satisfied are you with your present job skills?
37. Would you like to improve your present job skills?
38. What type of training would you like to have?
39. I would be willing to get additional education or training. . . . (Choose one or two.)

    ____(1) if I could find someone to care for my child or children
    ____(2) if I would have enough time to do the course work
    ____(3) if I had transportation
    ____(4) if I can study at my own pace
    ____(5) if I had the money or could get a loan
    ____(6) I don't want any more education or training

40. What kind of things now hold you back from getting more training or education?
41. In each blank fill in the number of hours you could spend going to some kind of school or training program.
42. What is the amount of money you would spend to get more training?
43. Has anyone ever suggested that you have a drinking problem?
44. My main reason for drinking is. . . .

45. How often do you use alcohol?
46. How many of your friends use alcohol?
47. The use of alcohol has caused most problems with which of the following?
48. If you were classified as having a drinking problem, what kind of professional treatment do you feel would be best?

    ____(1) in-patient care

    ____(2) out-patient facility

    ____(3) alcoholics anonymous program

    ____(4) alcohol counseling program (physician, counselor, etc.)

    ____(5) I don't know

49. What type of drugs do you use, if any?
50. My main reason for taking drugs is. . . .
51. How often do you use drugs?
52. Do your friends use drugs?
53. Has the use of drugs caused problems with any of the following?
54. Which best describes your record of felony convictions, not counting the offense for which you are under supervision?
55. Which best describes your record of misdemeanor convictions, not counting the offense for which you are under supervision?

If you have any criticisms or comments concerning the questionnaire, questions, services of probation and parole officers, or services you feel you should receive, please write it on the back of this page.

FORM C-6.
OFFENDER ASSIGNMENT
QUESTIONNAIRE

COURT REFERRAL PROGRAM
Volunteer Bureau
of Alameda County, California

Name _____ Date _____

The choice of your volunteer job depends on your interests, your skills, where you live and what transportation you have, what hours you can work, how many hours you will be giving, and what's needed in the community. To help us work out the best assignment with you, please answer the following questions:

I. Suppose you were placed at an agency called the East Bay Service Center. Mark your first, second, and third choices of jobs.

_____help the teacher of a class of three-year-olds

_____paint a room in the annex in bright colors for a new recreation room

_____answer the phones in the office

_____visit with an old woman who doesn't participate in the senior activities

_____coach a sports team for a youth club

_____help prepare and serve lunch for a preschool

_____type and file letters for the director

_____weed a garden and fix up a playground

_____tutor an eight-year-old who is having trouble with math

_____read to a blind college student

_____make stuffed animals for a preschool

_____help run a party in a senior citizen's center

_____assist with a field trip for retarded young adults

_____help stuff envelopes for a big mailing

_____general cleanup of office and classrooms

_____other

II. Check as many of the following as fit you.

I like to work

_____outdoors

_____with people

_____with teenagers

_____with people like me

_____in a large office

in busy surroundings

indoors

_____with paperwork

_____with the disabled

_____with animals

in quiet surroundings

_____with my hands

_____with small children

_____with the elderly

_____in a small office

III. I can get to these areas to do my volunteer work:

_____Albany

_____North Berkeley

_____Downtown Berkeley
_____West Berkeley
_____South Berkeley
_____Berkeley Hills
_____Emeryville
_____North Oakland
_____West Oakland
_____Downtown Oakland
_____East Oakland (Lake Merritt to High St.)
_____East Oakland (High St. to San Leandro)
_____Oakland Hills
_____Alameda
_____San Leandro

IV. I am available for volunteer work
(Check day, write in hours)

_____Monday_____
_____Tuesday_____
_____Wednesday_____
_____Thursday_____
_____Friday_____
_____Saturday_____
_____Sunday_____

V. I must depend on public transportation to
get around _____Yes _____No

VI. I have the following skills I could use in
volunteer work:
(Check as many as you wish.)

_____typing (words per minute_____)
_____filing
_____reception (answering phones)

_____gardening/landscape
_____carpentry
_____plumbing
_____electrical work
_____painting
_____plastering
_____carpet laying
_____janitorial
_____cooking
_____other maintenance/repairs
   (please list)_____
_____photography or printing
_____art work (making signs, posters)
_____sewing (and have a sewing machine)
_____knitting or crocheting
_____play a musical instrument:_____
_____other skill in the arts:_____

professional skills:_____

I could help teach
_____sport (please list)_____
_____arts/crafts (please list)_____
_____dance/theater (please list)_____
_____reading
_____basic math
_____other (please list)_____

VII. _____I prefer to finish my assignment as
         quickly as possible.
     _____I can stretch it out over several
         weeks.

INDEX